NO-NONSENSE MANAGEMENT

"This is a book designed to make managers think. The practical, meaningful statements are excellent reminders to the growing manager about how to be more effective. I am sure that this book will stimulate a great deal of positive action on the part of those who read it."

—Warren C. McGovney,
Vice President, Advanced Management Institute

"The most valuable and perhaps the only help which a potential manager gets from the written word is to be provoked. *No-Nonsense Management* is provocative in a readable, easily understood manner. It will provoke a potential manager and help in his self analysis."

—Allen P. Stults,
Chairman of the Board, The American National Bank

"The book provides meaningful advice for the aspiring General Manager and is a valuable refresher for those who have already made it. The short, punchy chapters make for easy reading and quick reference."

—Frank R. Beaudine,
President, Eastman & Beaudine, Inc.

No-Nonsense Management

A General Manager's Primer

Richard S. Sloma

BANTAM BOOKS
TORONTO · NEW YORK · LONDON · SYDNEY

NO-NONSENSE MANAGEMENT

A Bantam Book / published by arrangement with
Macmillan, Inc.

PRINTING HISTORY

Macmillan edition published October 1977
7 printings through May 1980

A Selection of Executive Program, July and October 1977, September
1978; Fortune, January 1978 and Playboy, August and September
1978.

Bantam edition / July 1981

ISBN 0-553-20035-6

Published simultaneously in the United States and Canada

PRINTED IN THE UNITED STATES OF AMERICA

0 9 8 7 6 5 4 3 2

This book is lovingly dedicated to my wife, Dee. Over the span of a quarter century she, more than anyone else, has taught me by her example that excellent results can indeed be achieved by the prudent and consistent application of dictatorial techniques.

Contents

We never understand a thing so well, and make it our own, as when we have discovered it for ourselves.
René Descartes

No-Nonsense Management

1

Welcome to the Club!

A "MODERN" MANAGER, browsing in the "business books" section of a local bookstore, might pick up this volume and, after leafing through a few pages, wonder how someone so "not with it" had the nerve to write a book on management.

After all, what kind of manager could write that "it is too easy to sympathize and empathize"? What can you say about someone who argues that "you must become callous to appeals that sound like 'He failed to achieve the objectives, but he really worked very hard,'" because "the hard business-world facts of life are that *no* rewards at all are granted for effort; they are granted *only* for results"?

"That kind of thinking went out with the 1950s," our browser might argue. But he'd be wrong. Because every word, every dictum in this book is part and parcel of a management style based on the utmost true respect for the men and women who make up the modern business organization.

But just as important to that style is an understanding and respect for the role of leadership. Today, it almost seems that managers feel they have to apologize for what they're paid to do—lead.

Effective management, that is, management which enhances the enduring value of invested capital, is equivalent to directive management. The leader simply must *lead*—that is, he must consistently and decisively *act* in accordance with a set of basic doctrines and principles.

It isn't all that difficult to lead. Except for rarities, people *expect* to be led. In fact, virtually every man needs a leader. And as much as people may express a yearning for liberty, such expressions come only when everything is going well. But let the first storm cloud appear on the horizon, and the vast majority of people will seek out a leader—someone who will tell them what to do, when to do it, and how to do it.

That's what most people don't understand about leadership—and why, when they read in this book that "it is too easy to sympathize and empathize," they feel such a philosophy isn't in touch with the times. If it seems that way, it's because these are times when many so-called leaders have tried to substitute the *trappings* of human relations for an understanding of and appreciation for human needs.

What are the most important things you, as a manager, can give your staff? One would certainly be an honest, open environment in which they can grow. Such growth demands understanding of and praise for people's successes; but it also requires a frank, honest appraisal of their mistakes and shortcomings. Too many managers fall short when it comes to the second half of that dictum; they can't bring themselves to tell a subordinate that he or she isn't cutting it, so they begin to look for "explanations" or "reasons" for failure. It really *is* too easy to sympathize and empathize, and it's damned hard to honestly appraise.

Another thing you must give your people is a strong company wherein they can prosper and find long-term success. It's wonderful if you can tell yourself that you're using an "enlightened approach" when you don't deal decisively with failure, but what have you done to all the other people in your organization? How many failures can you tolerate before you end up closing your doors and putting *all* of your people out of work?

And what about the person you don't "deal with" after a major failure? Are you serving *his* best interests when you don't "lay it on the line" and let him either salvage his career or start another one? Are you being honest with him—or with yourself?

This honesty, then, is what all the talk about the human equation boils down to, but I'm afraid that many managers feel uncomfortable with such honesty. As a result, they've subverted it to today's reliance on the form and trappings, not the substance, of good management.

Good management, effective management, means that you must be ready to state what to do and when to do it, but must studiously avoid assertions of how to do it.

If you fall into that trap, the work performed is yours. You won't have delegated; you'll have demoted yourself from general manager to doer.

More importantly, the time demands involved in monitoring the *how* details will absorb time and attention better spent on *what* and *when* decisions and follow-up. So while involving yourself in the *how* details may seem to provide you with a "security blanket" or an erroneous sense of indispensability, you'll find that the next required *what* and *when* activities will have been initiated too late, if at all, and your next *how* activity will be how to find a new job.

There is another trap you must worry about: sufficiently large doses of education and training will immobilize an aspiring manager. You become so aware of potential problems, of the many sides to a story, that you become confused. You make bland decisions, because "you don't yet have all the data." But blandness has never been an ingredient of effective management.

This book enumerates, defines, and elaborates on those rules of conduct which general managers must adhere to if they are to be effective. It seeks to so jar the reader from his or her mental lethargy that s/he will never again drift; s/he will never be labeled as having only "great potential." S/he will be an *achiever*. It is aimed specifically at general managers and those who, for misguided or unintelligible reasons, aspire to be general managers.

But what exactly is a "general manager"? That title can and does mean different things in different organizations. As used in this book, a general manager is the "top man" responsible for the major functions an organization-marketing, sales, operations (production, purchasing, maintenance, etc.), engineering, finance accounting, and personnel. He is sometimes called Chief Executive Officer, President, Vice-President–General Manager, Plant Manager, Vice-President, or simply General Manager. By a "functional manager" we mean the person who is responsible for the marketing function, the sales function, or any other specific function.

There are more than enough books for functional managers, and while they may find this volume valuable, they are not my prime target. The really big problem for an individual occurs when he is suddenly labeled "general manager." The change in behavior that is required is abrupt and traumatic. Promotions within one functional specialty usually entail only a larger amount of an already familiar activity: the guideposts are essentially the same, the priorities aren't all that dissimilar, and the landscape is about the same, only with a bit wider horizon. But one Monday morning, you enter an office with the title "General Manager" on the door. You know you must *do* something, you must *act*. But do what, and act how? Owners expect certain things of you, as do employees, but *what* things? This book will answer both those questions—or at least get you started at answering them.

The way you read this book is up to you. You can, as Alice was instructed, "start at the beginning and when you get to the end, stop." Or, you can dip into it at almost any point and suffer no loss of continuity at all. I do suggest that you scan the table of contents until you find a maxim or two that pique your interest, and then read those sections to get the flavor of the book. If you don't find any at all that arouse even a modicum of interest, you should not have bought this book, and you probably don't even belong in the business world.

The principles contained in this book, if properly grasped and implemented, will unleash stored-up talent in unprecedented quantities. You will gain "management momentum" as you implement more and more of these maxims; you will find them to be reinforcing and self-perpetuating. Conflict between these maxims, you'll soon discover, is inescapable; at one time or another, you'll hit a problem that demands a trade-off of emphasis from one to another of them in order to keep an organization intact.

There is no doubt that what aspiring general managers need more than ever today is a neo-Harvardian assertion of basic, irrefutable dogma to counterbalance the dilutive tendencies coherent in ill-conceived and unachievable "social" goals, and to help them regain the vibrancy and enthusiasm of an individual with purpose. The free world still finds its strength in individuals; in fact, individualism is the cornerstone of the free world.

The world of top-level management belongs to the bold, to those who have intellectual and personal courage and uncommon honesty. Are you one of them? Let's find out!

2

If You Want to Be a General Manager, Begin Performing Like a General Manager.

THAT'S RIGHT—just do it. The key to being named a general manager is to be recognized as general-manager material by those who can make that appointment. They must be convinced that your abilities exceed your record of successful performance. They must first be convinced that you can make the transition from functional to general excellence. A key question they'll ask is, "Can you reorient your efforts from the pursuit of *functional* goals to that of the *firm's* goals?"

The most effective way to convince them is to *demon-*

strate that you can. Translate your functional goals into terms that bear directly on the firm's goals.

- Don't just achieve your goal to increase market share; spell out how that will mean a greater return on the owner's investment.
- Don't just reduce expenses; rather, improve profit per share, cash flow, cash flow percentage of employed assets, and return on stockholders' equity.
- Don't just reduce accounts receivable; instead, reduce the asset base of the firm, improve return on assets, and increase cash flow and the cash flow percentage of employed assets.
- Don't merely commit yourself to keep engineering expenses within budget; instead, increase market share and gross margin by developing new products. Reduce the asset base by standardizing or substituting materials or parts.
- Don't just reduce purchasing costs; improve pre-tax profit and return on stockholders' equity. Increase cash flow by successful negotiation of extended pay terms.
- Don't just increase labor productivity; reduce product costs to improve earnings per share through a greater return on sales.
- Don't merely perform maintenance; prevent capital expenditures so as to reduce the asset base and improve cash flow.
- Don't just improve product quality; improve earnings per share by both increasing sales and obtaining a greater return on all sales.

In short, the more you think and act like a general manager, the more likely you'll be thought of as one. Be eager to take on more responsibility.

3

Never Tolerate Mediocrity.

YOUR JOB AS general manager is to achieve excellent results. Your superiors expect that of you. Your entire organization hopes that you'll be successful, because through *your* success, you assure *their* future.

If you're going to achieve excellent results, not only must you perform excellently, but so must level upon level of your organization. *Your people must identify you with an expectation of high levels of performance.* The minute you accept mediocrity, you lower the performance levels of your entire organization.

This rule is probably the most difficult rule to consistently and persistently apply. As you remain with an organization, you begin to establish business friendships.

You face the temptation of being excessively understanding of the many problems subordinates face. *It is too easy to sympathize and empathize.*

Unswerving enforcement of this demand for excellent performance will lead to unpleasant circumstances. There will be people who won't understand and, despite your best efforts at communication, never will understand *why* you set the levels of performance you do. But it isn't necessary that they all understand! You run the risk of becoming ineffective if you waste time attempting to achieve 100% understanding in your organization. "Understanding per share" is a datum neither sought nor reported.

You cannot expect more in performance or commitment than you yourself are willing to deliver. Therefore, the yearning for excellence, the drive for improvement, and the commitment to seek out more responsibility must start with you. But once it does, then it is not only fair and appropriate but *expected* that you will demand similar levels of performance on the part of everyone in your organization.

You must become callous to appeals that sound like "He failed to achieve the objectives, but he really worked very hard." The hard business-world facts of life are that *no* rewards at all are granted for effort; they are granted *only* for results. Results are never published as effort per share. Only earnings per share draw any interest, and mediocre earnings per share are of no interest at all.

If you allow your organization to perform with mediocrity, you will be labeled—accurately—a mediocre general manager.

4

Move Fast with Reversible Decisions—Move Less Fast with Irreversible Decisions.

COMMITTING ONESELF TO a decision is too often an occasion for agonizing. Learn to differentiate between those decisions you can reverse and those you can't. If you fail to attain the desired results, can you nullify the decision and restore conditions to those that obtained before?

Thus, a change in the organizational reporting relationship is reversible. Termination of an individual isn't. Decisions run the gamut from totally reversible to totally irreversible. Most decisions are gray—they embody elements of both reversibility and irreversibility.

When you move fast with a reversible decision, make sure you have alerted those that it will affect that it is reversible, and that it will be reversed if certain results aren't achieved within a stated time period. This is critical, because you want your people to give 100% when you make your move. If they know your decision is reversible, they'll give you that 100%. If they don't know that you'll restore things to the way they were if the move proves wrong, they'll hold back.

It's equally important to establish your expectancy of similar behavior from subordinates. The tempo or pace of an organization is directly proportional to the dispatch with which your subordinates treat the reversible decisions and the speed with which irreversible decisions are brought to higher organizational levels with recommendations for action.

5

Never Try to Solve All of the Problems All at Once—Make Them Line Up One-by-One.

WHEN YOU TRY TO attack a single problem you really face a number of problems. The sign of an amateur or freshman general manager is that he attempts to solve *all* of the problems at hand at the same time. His attack perimeter becomes increasingly large until, finally, his logistics requirements for solving the problems ex-ce~~ his conceptual capacity. He will fail.

The reason you were hired or promoted is that the company does have problems. The only reason that general managers are required at all is that there *are* problems. Successful managing of problem arrays is the discernible factor that differentiates the amateur or freshman general manager from the seasoned professional.

One of the reasons it's particularly difficult to cope with problem arrays is that the problems won't stand still. They continually change—in subject matter, in severity, in duration, or in scope.

The professional general manager learns to forget the adage "Look at the forest, not at the trees." He concentrates on the trees and the forest, too. That sounds difficult, and of course it is. To be excellent at anything, including general management, you pay a significant price. There's a demand for commitment that rises as your position of responsibility rises in the organization.

Because time is your most important asset, parcel it out grudgingly and wisely. Problems can be handled if you consider them one at a time—because then you can match each problem with an appropriate time unit. You can devote your total attention during that time unit to finding the best solution to that problem.

Pardon the cliché, but General Custer could have become one of our most famous military heroes if, somehow, he could have forced the Sioux nation to attack over the hill one at a time. Supremacy of the seas was guaranteed for the British when Lord Nelson maximized and exploited the technique of "crossing the 'T'" so as to allow *all* of his ships to fire broadside at *each* enemy ship as it appeared next in line. Look at problems as adversaries. Summon all your forces and deal with them one at a time. You'll never be overwhelmed.

6

Never Waste Time on Low-Impact Matters.

NEVER SQUANDER your limited time on matters that can generate only marginal or minimal return. As a general manager, you must take whatever steps are appropriate to ensure that you spend your time *only* in those areas and on those subjects which affect the organization *as a whole*—particularly those that affect profits.

This is an exceedingly difficult requirement to meet, and while it seems to make all the common sense in the world, no one in your organization will see to it that you meet it except you. And sometimes even you will be your own worst enemy. You will tend, for example, to give too much time to those problems you're most familiar with. If your functional specialty was, say, marketing, you'll be tempted to spend too much time on marketing problems.

This is a trap that a freshman general manager often falls into. He desperately wants to avoid failure in his first time at bat, so he tries to stay with those areas in which he feels he has a better-than-even chance of success.

On the other hand, if the firm's primary problem is indeed in marketing, then a general manager must be equally careful not to *avoid* involvement because he's fearful of falling into this particular trap.

After you have enumerated the problems facing your organization, select those that truly affect the entire firm and rank the problems so that you can, in turn, rank your time. Seek out the high-impact problems, and give preference to short-term rather than long-term problems. They are easier to solve, and their solution guarantees your continued presence to face the longer-term problems.

The primary criterion for ranking impact must necessarily be effect on profits. Given two problems—one which involves increasing sales and another which involves increasing profits—always choose the profit problem as first priority. Unless profits in the coming quarters are assured, you simply will not be the general manager in the coming years.

There will be times when lower-level management people will "send a problem upstairs" simply because they are afraid of dealing with it. Mind you, it will never be presented that way to you. Almost certainly, it will be presented as an appeal for "counsel and guidance." But counsel and guidance are far down the list of components of your job description. The most compelling parts of that job description always discuss results, always discuss performance, and are always expressed in profits, earnings per share, and return on assets. Do not allow flattery to reorder the priorities that you have established for yourself or for the organization.

7

Don't Even Listen to Any Significant Program Presentation That Doesn't Include a Definite Time Period Allocated for Planning.

WITH ONLY THE RAREST OF exceptions, a program fails—i.e., does not achieve (or exceed) the targeted results—not because it is conceptually unsound or tries to achieve unattainable goals, but because someone did a miserable job in the area of planning. Either important tasks were entirely overlooked, or it was merely assumed that, somehow, they'd be reasonably well performed.

With respect to every significant program, withhold

your approval until the accountable individuals have presented a complete and detailed plan of implementation and achievement. Insist that this plan include a reasonable time period allocated for complete and detailed planning.

Former Secretary of State Dr. Henry Kissinger was known for, among many other things, his insistence on excellence in planning documentation. An aide, who had submitted a plan to him several days prior, asked Dr. Kissinger what he thought of it. Dr. Kissinger mildly asked "Is this the best plan that you can devise?" "Well," hesitated the aide, "I'm sure with a little more work it would be better." Whereupon, Dr. Kissinger returned the plan to him.

After almost two more weeks of effort the aide resubmitted the improved plan. Several days later, Dr. Kissinger called the aide into his office. "Is this really the best plan that you recommend?" Taken slightly aback, the aide mumbled that, "perhaps a point or two could be better defined—perhaps more direct accountability . . ." The aide left the office, plan under his arm, determined that he would develop a plan that anyone—even Henry Kissinger—would recognize as "perfect."

The aide worked day and night for the next three weeks, on occasion even sleeping in his office! Finished! He proudly strode into Dr. Kissinger's office, handed the plan to the Secretary, and braced himself for the inevitable, "Is this really the *very* best plan that you can come up with?" "Yes sir, Mr. Secretary!" the aide exclaimed. "Good," said Dr. Kissinger, "in that case, I'll read it!"

A number of lessons for our budding effective general manager. Subordinates *can* do better if they believe that you *expect* them to. Mediocrity was *not* acceptable. Don't bother even reading "non-excellent" plans. Signal the organization that *only* excellence and thoroughness *are* expected and accepted.

8

First Be Effective; Then Devise Ways to be Efficient.

THE EFFECTIVE general manager must first improve return on investment. Second, he must improve return on investment. The third step, failing the first two, is to update his résumé, placing strong emphasis on "policy differences with superiors."

The problem with efficiency improvement activity is that it is always time-consuming. There are always many ways to achieve the same end. The definition of alternatives alone takes time. Much additional time is consumed in evaluation of and selection among the defined alternatives.

The effective general manager must have the ability to quickly identify the *one* course of action which will *assuredly* generate profit improvement. He then acts *without* documenting other possibilities. He first and foremost ensures projected results; then, and only then, does he worry about how to do it more easily, more cheaply, or even sooner.

A tempting fallacy says that if we first concentrate on efficiency, effectiveness must necessarily follow. The fatal flaw is that you will run out of time before you achieve effectiveness. Effectiveness is equated with objective achievement. Usually, you will be in pursuit of only one objective, or, perhaps, of several closely related objectives. Also, usually, there are innumerable ways to achieve your objective.

Efficiency is concerned with the manner or technique employed to reach the goal. Achieving it demands measuring and evaluating each of the many available alternatives. Thus, far too much time will pass, destroying the opportunity for objective achievement.

The effective squadron commander will complete the bombing of a key target despite alarmingly high mortality rates rather than fail to knock out the target but keep casualties at an all-time low.

9

Seek Out Those Rare Individuals Who Are Truly Committed, and Build Around Them.

THE MOST IMPORTANT function in a company is the personnel function." How many times have we heard this principle given lip service! But how few times do we see it observed in practice! The personnel function is the most important function, but only in the sense that it recruits, procures, pirates, or steals the individuals that the firm needs.

A business organization's results are directly traceable to the individuals who make up that organization. It has been true, it is true, and it will forever be true that "a good man is hard to find." So one of your top-priority activities as general manager must be to constantly assess individuals in your organization and outside it, to seek out those rare individuals who are genuinely committed to success, and then—⟨and this is the crux of the matter—⟩ *to build around them.* You must provide an incessant flow of opportunity enlargement at all management levels so that seasoned managers will emerge. Those individuals will become the cornerstone of the corporate growth to which you must be committed.

Success on the football field, for example, is really won or lost in the Player Personnel Office. Wins or losses begin with the selection of scouting personnel. The extent to which the scouts (or recruiters) are competent will determine the resulting team's ultimate success.

Carrying our analogy slightly further, the most successful teams tailor their strategy and tactics so as to effectively exploit the inherent strengths of particularly talented individuals. Examples are obvious. Aggressive, hard-charging offensive linemen pave the way for O. J. Simpson; while steadfast, blocking offensive linemen provide pocket security for "Broadway Joe" Namath and Fran Tarkenton. The principle is aggressively practiced by successful business general managers.

10

It Never Pays to Delay
Personnel Decisions.

THE MEASURE OF your performance is the sum of
the results achieved by all of the individuals in your
organization. Therefore, as you review the performance
of those individuals, you must distinguish between those
who are obtaining results and those who are not. In both
cases, it is incumbent upon you to *do* something.

The individual who is obtaining results must be viewed
as a logical candidate for an upward move. You must
present him with broader and more intensive challenges
and opportunities. Do not try to prejudge whether he will

or will not be successful; put him in the position, and
allow the results to speak for themselves.

In an effectively administered Management By Objectives (MBO) environment, an individual will know
if he is obtaining the desired results; you won't have to
tell him. Since he knows, he will *expect* to be presented
with a greater opportunity for displaying his talents. A
delay in promotion will dampen his respect for his superiors; he will seek greater opportunities outside your
organization. You'll lose him.

On the other hand, if an individual *isn't* obtaining results, not only is *he* aware of it, but so are his peers and
subordinates. If you allow him to remain in his position,
you are signaling to your organization that it is okay to
fail to perform. The underachievers will heave a sigh of
relief, while the overachievers will seek out other organizations, in which *their* results *will* be recognized.

Never try to salvage an individual. By the time an individual is in his thirties or forties, he is what he will be.
Remember, *you* are measured by "earnings per share,"
not "converts per year."

11

It Is Better to Impose Slight
Over-control than to Lose Control.

EFFECTIVE CONTROL means that no significant decision (affecting dollars, people, equipment, and so forth) is made without the general manager's knowledge and concurrence. Because a business organization is a dynamic entity, your control will continually be tested. Some of the testing is generated by the changing requirements and environments of your firm. Another portion is generated by the individuals of your organization, who, out of whatever motivations, may seek to pursue self-serving courses of action.

It is inescapable that you as general manager are responsible for the viability of your firm. You simply *must* be aware of major or potentially major decisions. You must be involved. To paraphrase a recent television commercial, "When you are responsible for something, how much should you know about it?" The answer is that you should know precisely as much as is necessary to successfully meet your obligations as general manager. The ultimate penalty for failure to install and consistently enforce controls is failure to achieve objectives —and, consequently failure to achieve tenure. It is in the firm's best interests and in yours too, therefore, that you be perhaps slightly too deeply involved in the "sign-off" process than too little involved.

12

It Is Easier to Remove Controls (or Ease Them) than It Is to Install Them.

WHEN YOU INSTALL your control system be sure that, if anything, it is somewhat tighter than necessary. If it is only somewhat tighter than necessary, there will be no inordinate adverse reaction on the part of subordinates; but if your control system is insufficient, you will have no alternative but to subsequently tighten it. Then subordinates *will* register adverse reactions; partly because they will resent further intrusions and partly because they will sense that you really aren't the sure-of-yourself leader that they expected. Their faith in you will have suffered.

If, however, after slight overcontrol initially, you subsequently loosen a few restraints, your managerial effectiveness will increase. Strong initial control will assert your management prerogatives, and you'll be respected for it. Subsequent loosening will be interpreted as a gesture of faith in and respect for your subordinates. Further, your subordinates will endorse your tempering adjustments because you will have demonstrated wisdom and understanding—and excellent insight. "After all," they'll say, "we *are* capable and he recognized it."

Be sure that your initial control program is based upon well-known needs of the firm. The basic need is for improvement in earnings per share. Your control program must be identified with that need; it must never be perceived as an effort to serve a personal whim. Maximum neutralization of opposition will be achieved to the extent that you are successful in identifying your control program as responsive to the *firm's* objectives.

13

The Shorter the Control Cycle, the More Effective the Results.

SURROUNDING EVERY significant decision is an aura of circumstances, conversation, nuances, balanced conflicting interests and opinions, and so on. However careful the documentation is, it will fail to capture the "flavors" of the decision. They'll be remembered only as long as a matter of greater importance fails to displace them in your memory.

Subordinates are rarely impressed by what you *say*, but they are deeply impressed by what you *do*. It is one thing to *say*, "I am exercising control," but quite another to actually exercise it.

A control cycle is the time it takes to conceive, document, approve, implement, and assess the results of a decision. The longer the control cycle, the greater the likelihood that an intervening development will distract control focus. In that event you won't firmly exercise control, and you'll have performed a negative action. You will have *failed* to do. Your subordinates, taking your cue, will respond accordingly.

For many decisions however, the control cycle must be lengthy. The way to deal with such a control cycle is to segmentize it, so that you can demonstrate effective control by controlling steps or phases of the total program. Gantt charts, "milestones," and so on are useful tools by which to monitor progress and preclude major surprises.

Make sure that the control review points are meaningful and relevant. They should reflect the major, self-contained portions of program activity, whether these are contained wholly within one function or extend through two or more. Of particular interest is the point at which different functions—marketing and research engineering, research engineering and production engineering, cost accounting and product management, and so on—interface.

Make sure that individuals, not departments, are identified and accountable. When all other measures are inappropriate, calendar dates can always be used.

14

No One Ever Gives 100% All the Time.

IT'S EASY TO MAKE that statement, or even to get a bunch of managers to agree to it; it's quite another thing to motivate subordinates so that they perform more effectively because they want to come closer to their potential. While trying to motivate subordinates, do not, ever, try to become a practicing psychologist. It is *not* important that you understand or agree with *why* a particular individual is "turned on"; it's only important that he *is* "turned on."

The best way that you can provide appropriate motivational leadership is to push the limits of your own imagination and innovation so that you generate a stream of ever-expanding challenges for subordinates. As they move from one achievement to another, they will realize that they are growing and developing. Reinforced confidence will propel them still faster, and eventually those who truly want to be excellent, who want *your* job, will begin to generate their own stream of challenges.

In business, as in life, perfection is only approached, never reached. But the *struggle* toward perfection is the very essence of success in business, and in life. That struggle involves, on occasion, letting go of the tree trunk with both hands and going out on a limb. It is what provides life, and work, with color, vibrancy, dash, and vigor.

The business world belongs to the quick. It is the one prerequisite you must have if you are ever to savor the tantalizingly delicious taste of success or the reinvigorating agony of defeat. The way we attack and cope with that struggle is the ultimate measure of us all.

15

Aggressive and Consistent Review of Accountability Guarantees an Improvement in Results.

THERE ARE REALLY FIVE separate precepts bound together in this principle. The first is found in the words "aggressive" and "consistent." If this book has *any* lasting effect on you, I hope you'll remember that a general manager *must* know where his organization is at and where it's headed. The *only* way to know that is to review interim or milestone results. Furthermore, the review process must be in a *quantitative* mode. Adjectives and adverbs are appropriate only *after* numbers describe the real-world circumstances; they're useful only if they convey prognoses for good or ill.

The third precept is implied in the notion of "accountability." The presumption is that a relatively effective MBO program is in place and thriving. That being so, individuals can perform at their best only if they are regularly, formally, and *objectively* measured. That process is the essence of accountability.

The fourth precept is that embodied in the word "guarantee." Guided by the first three precepts, you will either deliver on your gurantees, or you'll soon be asked to seek other employment.

The fifth precept is the unending emphasis placed upon results. In the business world, the worth of an individual is directly and proportional solely to the results that that individual generates.

16

The Effectiveness of a Firm's Planning and Control Is Inversely Related to the Organization Level at Which It Is Exercised.

THE CLOSER THAT accountability approaches the "doer," the better—i.e., the more effective—will be overall performance. Dollars and minutes are expended hundreds of times, even thousands of times, per day by fourth- fifth-, and lower-level organizational personnel. If planning and control are taken seriously only at the top levels of the organization, commitments will be made of large sums of money and time but the odds of successful realization of plans will be almost nil. And if goals *are* achieved, it will only further attest to the even better results that might have been attained.

A firm's performance is the sum of the thousands of relatively small transactions within it that occur daily. Returns and allowances are granted or denied one at a time. Freight expenses are incurred individually, shipment by shipment. Products are made one by one; sales calls are individual events. And so on and so forth.

The value to managerial control of controllable/uncontrollable accounting and non-accounting reporting, therefore, increases geometrically as they penetrate the layers of an organization. The more knowledge you gain of the processing of these individual transactions, the greater the benefits of self-monitoring.

Inspection of one's performance by one's peers is one of the most effective prods to productivity that there is. In fact, it is the *only* effective prod—other than inspection by one's superior. There's no more effective guarantee of peer surveillance than a firm-wide reporting system which strips away the possibility of concealment of one's performance. An awareness that your performance *will* be visible to your peers and superiors ensures either an acceptable level of performance or the individual's termination.

17

Never Accept a "Numbers Only" Financial Report; Insist on Prose: "Good–Bad" Statements and Prognoses.

TOO OFTEN YOU WILL FIND that subordinates try to fulfill only the letter of their accountability and scrupulously avoid the spirit. They know that you insist on maintaining a numbers-oriented discipline, so in their effort to escape vulnerability, they respond by providing more raw-numbers data than you can possibly digest.

The first time that you accept a "raw data" report and do the analytical and comparative homework yourself, you will have taken the first, irretrievable step away from being a general manager and toward demotion to a "doer."

Numbers reports will come from many sources. A cost report will accurately present all of the numbers in exhaustively complete detail, but will fail to tell you, in so many words, that the new product or project should be abandoned. A productivity report from the industrial engineering department will present last week's data but will omit the year-to-date comparative statements that should lead to specific action directives to individual foremen.

While business logic and decisions are based on numbers, business management and action are based on adjectives and adverbs. Insist that subordinates *always* cover numbers reports with judgmental statements. Furthermore, insist that prognoses based upon the symptoms revealed by the numbers be made. You'll not only be better informed—and, therefore, a better general manager—but you will at the same time be taking positive action toward developing stronger subordinates.

18

Manage Inventories and
Receivables by "Profile" Too,
Not Only in Total.

A TYPICAL DIRECTIVE from a general manager
who is running scared is a bald "cut the inventory."
Lacking conditions and qualifications, such a directive
(if his subordinates pursue it seriously) will certainly
lead to a reduction all right, but it will inevitably be the
wrong items that are cut—by the wrong amounts and
at the wrong times.

If inventory *must* be cut on a crash basis, only the "A"
items (those which represent the highest total cost) will
be affected. You'll reduce quantities on purchase orders

and postpone deliveries, and you'll get your reduction this month. However, shipments *next month* will be jeopardized, which will lead to further profit erosion, which will lead to further inventory and production cuts, which will lead, eventually, to *liquidation*, the *ultimate* reduction of inventory—and of receivables, too.

So don't concentrate on *total* inventory; it is far more valuable to know where, in the production/marketing process, segments of inventory are invested. Thus, the inventory "profile" to be managed is defined by the relative amounts of raw material, work-in-process, and finished goods. *The rule to follow is that proportionately more inventory dollars should be invested in finished goods as the engineering content of the finished goods approaches zero.* Conversely, proportionately, more inventory dollars should be invested in raw materials as the engineering content (the amount of engineering expense in the product cost) of the finished goods increases.

The less engineering content per unit of marketable product, the more important availability becomes as a buying influence. This is particularly true for industrial products, because the smaller the engineering content of the product, the lesser the preplanning that's exercised by the user in anticipating its replacement. The manufacturer who provides the most consistent availability will obtain the sale and, eventually, the greatest market share.

By the same token, accounts-receivable management must be more concerned with the age-"profile" and days-outstanding ratio than with total dollars. If all receivables are current and not in dispute, then the higher the dollar investment, the better. It is the age and consequent questionable collectibility of the receivables that will tell you when remedial action is needed.

In any event, always judge inventory and receivables investments in terms of meeting the requirements of the served market. There is no magic total or ratio which is always applicable to all industries. There is no question, however, that less is always better than more.

19

Rank Your Time and Project Selection According to Impact on Profitability.

THE FIRST EXPECTATION a firm's owners have is that you will see to it that the firm improves its profitability. The second duty you have is to see to it that the firm improves its profitability. Your third duty is also to see to it that the firm improves its profitability. If you fail to meet these three top-priority duties, you needn't concern yourself with lesser-priority ones. You won't be there to be bothered with them.

Frequently, corporate press releases pitifully speak warmly about increased morale or improved market share or increased sales or enhanced something-else. They can't report improvement in profits, so they struggle to say *something* "nice."

I have yet to see *Fortune* publish a "Top 500" ranked by morale per share or market share per share or sales dollar per share or something-else per share. What *is* reported and ranked and is of top interest to investors is *earnings* per share. Therefore, continually review your time commitments and your firm's projects (they absorb your subordinates' time)so as to ensure that you resolve or manage *first* those problems or activities with greatest impact on profitability.

However appealing another priority may be, failure to rank activities by impact on profitability will, at best, fail to optimize profitability for the firm; at worst, it will mean failing to earn any profit at all. The result? Your name will head a board-meeting agenda, with the action required by the board shown as "Form a committee to seek a replacement."

20

Manage an Organization as Nature Would: (A.) Show Neither Malice nor Pity. (B.) Abhor a Vacuum, Whether of Power or Action.

ALL HUMAN BEINGS are imperfect judges. The potential for error in judgment is proportional to the lack of qualification with which the issue is described. In other words, the greater the emotional involvement you have, the less likely that you will make a prudent judgment.

When managing an organization, you must inescapably manage *people*. And, abhorrent as it may seem to some sensibilities, you must, although only on occasion, manipulate people. If you allow yourself the luxury of granting pity or inflicting malice in your dealings with people, you are jeopardizing the authority which your subordinates have grudgingly granted you. You will quickly become known as a "great guy" to some, but as a prejudiced and emotional demigod to others. And you'll be known to *no one at all* as the general manager.

A void of inaction by subordinates will, if tolerated, soon lead to failure to achieve the desired results; therefore it *cannot* be tolerated. Be ever watchful for the first signs: postponed target dates, failure of an organizational unit to automatically and vigorously swing into a recoup program should a shortfall occur, and so forth. Once you recognize the symptoms, establish what you consider to be a reasonable time-to-act interval. If your subordinates fail to act in a timely manner, then leave your office, *personally* go to the scene of the action, *personally* convene the relevant personnel, and do not adjourn until *personally* measurable objectives have been established. Make a mental note to further "loosen the pin" of the individual who failed to act.

It is only as your subordinates see how, when, and why you personally take action when the firm faces a problem that they decide to award you more or less respect. You earn respect *only* by action; inaction earns only disrespect. If the general manager fails to fill a vacuum, either someone else (a new general manager) will fill it, or the firm will begin to fail.

21

Management's Responsibility to Employees Begins and Ends with Creating an Environment for Individual Opportunity.
(A.) Support Those Who Grasp It.
(B.) Replace, Promptly, Those Who Fail—for Whatever Reason —to Grasp It.

MANY RESPONSIBILITIES are thrust upon a general manager, including a critical set that relates to the firm's employees. Of course, responsibility for providing safe working conditions, preventing discrimination, and so on must be properly discharged.

Of utmost concern to us here, though, is simultaneously fulfilling your responsibility to improve return on investment (ROI) and your responsibility to so motivate individual members of your organization that they will achieve the return-on-investment objectives.

Your organization consists of individuals. Just as you carefully sift through your catalog of products or services to try to exactly match a customer's need, you must also continually sift through your organization so as to select those individuals who exactly match your organizational needs. There are only two ways you can identify such individuals.

One way is to simply "play God." Many managers do try to fill that role, ridiculous as it may seem. To "play God," you decide, all by yourself, what an individual's limits are. You simply sit there on your vinyl throne and prejudge. It is, unfortunately, an impossible role to fill, and the results of such a method usually reflect that.

The *effective* way (and also the more difficult way) is to consistently structure an organizational environment so that opportunity abounds for the expression of individual capabilities. When you first see evidence that one of your people is responding to a challenge, the reinforcement cycle will have been initiated. That individual, assured that his effort will be both recognized and supported, will seek out yet more ways to display his growing confidence. He will have been motivated—and he will as a result increase the firm's ROI. You will have discharged your responsibility to your subordinates, and your organization's results will improve. All you have to do is avoid the temptation to judge individuals by yourself; let their *performance* speak for them.

If some people don't respond to challenge, those individuals must be replaced. Don't divert time from ROI improvement efforts to try to understand *why* they are not responding; accept the fact that they are *not*. If you fail to replace those individuals promptly, you'll suffer two consequences you cannot afford. First, other subordinates will interpret your inaction as a signal that you approve of do-nothing performance. Second, and more important, those nonresponsive individuals will become a career block to their subordinates. The aggressive and ambitious individuals will leave to seek opportunities elsewhere. How many job applicants have you interviewed who listed "more opportunity" as the reason for their departure from previous employers?

22

Plan Your Operational
Environment Changes So That the
Implementation Periods Parallel
Each Other.

You AND YOUR ORGANIZATION get only one shot at
each day. If you, as general manager, fail to initiate an
appropriate number of growth programs, your organization is left unchallenged and you have failed to achieve
maximum results. It's a bit like the story of the farmer
who discovered that the yield from his 100-acre farm was
greater if all 100 acres were planted each year, rather
than each acre annually in turn.

The extent of simultaneity that you'll be able to put into effect is pretty much determined by your imagination and the capacity of your organization. Sure, you've got quite a few programs going at the same time, but too many general managers fail to see to it that the concurrently active planning programs all reach fruition *at the same time.* An organization can productively complete more planning projects in a given time period than implementation projects; this is true because of the greater control you can exercise over planning.

So your goal is a balanced blend of planning *and* implementation projects, with staggered finish-dates, so that all of the planning tasks are completed prior to the planned start of implementation programs, in sufficient quantity and complexity to require 110% of your organization's efforts.

23

Your True Adversary Is Time. Not Competition, Not Legislation, Not the Economy—but Time.

MANY FORCES AFFECT the growth and profitability of a firm. The action (or reactions) of competitors, new legislation, major economic trends, the health of the markets you serve, the costs of purchased materials and services—these are only a few of the forces over which you have virtually no control. The best you can do is try to anticipate developments and initiate steps so as to mitigate their impact. But it takes time to learn enough to make reasonable projections. It takes time to formulate response programs. It takes time to mobilize the organization to complete program planning and implementation. It takes time to monitor feedback from actions taken and consider modifications you should make.

We hear and read much today about the need to conserve the environment, conserve energy, and conserve resources. But the mark of a successful general manager is that, first and foremost, he conserves *time*. Not only *his* time, but the collective time of his organization. The first step in successful conservation of time is recognizing the importance of the thing you want conserved. That recognition is best won by a general manager who personally exhibits a sense of urgency.

If a thing is worth doing, it's not only worth doing well, but it also would have been worth *more* had it been done yesterday!

24

It Is Far Better to Risk
Over-investment of Time in
Productive Planning than to Rely
on Ad Hoc Solutions
to Unpredictable Problems.

Too OFTEN, THE URGE TO begin doing something
is so compelling that we fail to completely define just
what it is that we are about to do. Doing offers an im-
mediate tangibile satisfaction—results! We want to "get
on with it."

But as time passes in an organizational setting, pressure rapidly grows to see some visible or tangible results

of programs. Objectives are fairly easily defined—they are attractive and desirable. Owners or members of the board quickly fix those objectives in their corporate memory.

Since you're responsible for results, you, as general manager, run the risk of underestimating the implementation problems and overestimating your capability to overcome problems as they arise. If these *are* true growth programs, the implementation problems you'll face are, by definition, beyond your firm's collective experience.

A fixed amount of time exists between adoption of a program and the target date fixed for goal achievement. Only two functions can occupy that time. First, there's planning—anticipating problems and defining action for their resolution. Second, there's implementing. Productive, imaginative planning will always expedite the implementing. It takes time to plan, but it's time well spent.

A program is most vulnerable in its implementation stage—because of the many, varied, and uncontrollable forces which can deal fatal blows. It's better to miss the date for plan completion in order to ensure successful implementation than to prematurely launch your implementation without an adequate map and thereby miss the objective. Better for the owners, better for the firm, better for you.

25

Management Planning Is Not
Complicated, but It *Is* Tedious
—That's Why the Temptation
Is So Strong to Avoid It.

PLANNING IS an inglorious task—almost always
a "staff" function, something "we really should formalize" and "do more of." However, productive, meaningful
planning is *at least* as important as the challenge of
"doing."

Too often, we witness a "doer" who makes it look *so*
easy. We seldom witness his hours and hours of prepara-
tory planning. It's ridiculously easy to make on-the-spot

61

decisions—*if* you have previously thought out and evaluated all of the feasible alternatives.

Why, then, are we hesitant to seek out and perform planning tasks? The most salient aspect of planning is that it is an iterative process—that is, one must examine *all* the feasible alternatives and document possible scenarios so that, given any plausible eventuality, one has prepared a response that will lead to one's goal.

The initial task of enumerating the alternatives, not to mention that of evaluating each and determining satisfactory responses, is a painstaking, desk-bound activity. It's *so* much easier to attend an association meeting or seminar, tour the plant, make a customer call, or even expedite an order. Planning requires patience and perseverence beyond any "doing" action. You must check and recheck to make sure both that you've assigned the proper probability to the identified alternatives and that you've included all feasible alternatives. It's a tedious process—and no one, least of all a general manager, enjoys tedium.

26

Laws of Reversed Entropy Apply
to Business Organizations: That Is,
Energy Must Be Applied to the
System to Restore, Maintain,
or Increase Order. In the Absence
of Applied Energy, the System
Will Deteriorate Toward
Increasing Disorder.

UNLIKE NEWTON'S FIRST LAW, a business organization, once in motion, will not stay in uniform motion. Vagaries of the marketplace, action or inaction by competitors, regulatory changes, international developments, the consequences of political action or inaction, and certainly of top importance, changes in the individuals who make up an organization—all these forces and many more perturb the organization. If unchecked, they cause the motion of the organization to become chaotic.

Worse yet, a business organization, if not tended to, will increasingly fail to achieve notable results. A company cannot stand still. The inference is that if a company does not *progress*, it will *regress*. Just as there is validity to the product life-cycle curve (published many times, usually in chapter two or chapter three of a typical marketing-management treatise), so too is there validity in a *company* life-cycle curve. The similarities are numerous, but there's one major difference. *The company life-cycle curve is controllable—it need not decline.* The health and resilence of a firm are direct reflections of the vigor, enthusiasm, and imagination of its management—and, especially, of *you* as general manager.

Think of "turnaround" performance when sleepy or complacent management is replaced by new and eager management—think of those occasions as positive flexpoints on the company's life cycle curve. The extended absence of fresh inputs, properly timed, from various functional disciplines means that a firm will slowly but surely (it is inevitable) show declines first in ROI, then in new orders, then in backlog, then in sales, then, even worse, again in ROI, and then fail to invest (as a stopgap measure to avoid pressing cash problems), and so on and on toward oblivion.

The needs of a company vary as does the environment in which the company operates. No orchestra conductor would allow a single instrument to continuously dominate throughout a performance, yet how many general managers do you know who consistently emphasize only one functional element—say, sales? Without blending of functional disciplines, a company will react as does an individual—its response will diminish as the stimulus remains constant. Until, given enough time, all the agents of change will have taken their ultimate toll, and the organization can't respond at all.

27

Results Are Generated by
Conditions—viz., the Operating
Environment of a Firm. Don't
Expect Changes in Results if You
Haven't Changed the Conditions.

RESULTS, FINANCIAL AND OTHERWISE, are only the
consequences of the action and interaction of forces.
Some of these forces—people, products, plant, and policies—are under your direct control. By definition, the
forces of your competitors are not under your direct control. They exercise influence indirectly on your firm as
you do on theirs.

As general manager, you are expected to achieve different results from those posted previously. The only measure of results that counts is improvement in the firms profitability.

In a business environment, the best and most effective change is *orderly* change. The only way to achieve orderliness is to *plan* change as carefully and thoroughly as possible. The objective of planning must be to achieve or exceed a stated ROI, presumably one which is higher than that recorded in the firm's recent history. Once such a goal is established, you can begin to consider appropriate changes in the available resources: people, products, plant, and policies. It is not always necessary to effect early changes in all four resources. Rest assured, however, that one way or another, there will be changes in all four areas before too many years have passed.

Once the need for change is expressed in terms of specific goals for the firm, subordinates will recognize the need for change in their respective operating areas. They may still need further motivating in order to effect change, but they will, sometimes grudgingly, acknowledge the need for change. At this point, detailed plans from third- and lower-level managers can be finalized that will not only result in the desired changes, but will serve to measure and control interim progress as well.

The array of people, products, plant, and policies which you inherited produced certain results. Those results will be repeated in the short term if the array remains the same. But performance will erode in the long term if the array remains unchanged.

28

Get Time on Your Side.

TIME DOES, INDEED, go by. It proceeds as an endless chain. Effective use of time requires that you are "hooked onto" that chain rather than just observing its passing.

Every program or project requires a gestation period. You need time to obtain, analyze, and synthesize data, to "sell" a concept, to obtain delivery of services or products, and so on.

There are only two ways in which you can use time more productively. The first is to discover new techniques so that you can perform a given task in less time. As a general manager, this method will rarely be available to you. First of all, your job is essentially nonrepetitive;

you do not perform identical tasks over and over again.

The second way to use time more productively is to initiate concurrent actions so that many more programs are completed in the same time. Getting six elephants pregnant at the same time will not reduce the gestation period to one-sixth the usual time, but it will produce six times as many elephants in the same period of time. If complementary programs are launched simultaneously in the marketing, sales, engineering, accounting, operations, and purchasing areas, you will generate six times the improvement you could expect if they were initiated sequentially.

29

Only Rarely Are Business Failures or Poor Decisions the Result of *Too Much Planning;* Almost Universally They Can be Traced to Management Ego—the Temptation to Say, "I Don't Need a Plan; I'm Sure I Can Handle Whatever Develops."

THE MANAGER WHO MAKES on-the-spot decisions without insuring that adequate prior-planning has occurred in effect says, "I am sufficiently talented and have enough relevant experience so that my judgment can be trusted." But the alert subordinate usually thinks, "This guy shoots from the hip."

Too often, we fail to distinguish "paralysis by analysis" from adequate planning. The hip-shooter is quick to accuse subordinates of paralysis-by-analysis. Conversely, inadequate subordinates are quick to *practice* paralysis-by-analysis, cloaking it under a "need for thorough planning" veneer.

Management planning does not consist merely in the collection of data. It is an aggressive action: it seeks to take business from the competition and provide more value to the customer. Its premise is that the resultant action will take the firm into previously unexplored (or uncharted) areas. Its purpose is thus like the mission of the *Enterprise* in the television series "Star Trek"—"to boldly go where no firm has gone before."

Mobilization of the management group's collective knowledge and experience is always superior to (i.e., more effective and productive than) reliance upon one individual's judgment, especially in times of crisis. Reliance upon a thorough, well-documented and detailed map or plan significantly reduces the risk of unnecessary failure—if only by leading to the postponement of decisions that, if improperly or prematurely made, could quite possibly prove fatal to the firm.

30

When Management
Only *Responds* to Developments,
the Bell Has Begun to Toll.
Excellent Management
Predetermines Developments
and Thereby Controls
Its Corporate Future.

RECALL WHAT General Ulysses S. Grant said: "Be there firstest with the mostest." The philosophy of a winner! There is the story, too, of the zealous standard-bearer in the War Between the States who, leading the charge, suddenly found himself deep within enemy lines.

A voice called to him to come back and rejoin his friendly forces. "Hell," he replied, "Move up the troops!" The philosophy of a leader!

To grow and prosper, a firm must continuously expand the limits of its business environment. It must *lead*. One of the most succinct definitions of leadership is that a leader is an initiator of favorable change.

The firm that relies upon a defensive, "Maginot Line" attitude can assuredly expect an end-around attack—and subsequent defeat. The essence of the "stand pat" fallacy is that it will take longer than you imagined to regain the status quo. And while your firm is spending—and actually wasting—time and money trying only to catch up, your competitors are already formulating their next offensive thrust. When you are finally caught up, you won't, after all, find your competitors there—they'll have moved on, making further inroads into your diminishing business boundaries.

31

Management Control Is Like Vitamins: You Need a Fresh Dose Every Day to Stay Healthy; They Are Not Supplied Automatically.

MANAGEMENT CONTROL IS NOT an event—it is a *process*. It is a social, not mechanical, process, in that it is affected, favorably or otherwise, by the net vector sum of the behavioral characteristics of the individuals who constitute the group.

Every individual has this basic behavioral characteristic: he is subject to the principle of "diminishing response to a constant stimulus." Inescapably, in the

75

absence of new stimuli, whether from external or internal ("self-starting") sources, each individual becomes a little more lax, a little less disciplined, a little more out of control.

The general manager is the inevitable source of organization stimuli. The pace he sets, the example he shows, the communications he transmits will reveal the level of control his people can anticipate. Indeed, they will indicate whether *any* level of effective control will be sustained.

A business firm can no more store up a "supply" of management control than a human being can store up a supply of vitamins. The vigor of management control is lessened with each and every one of the hundreds of assaults made on it daily, on the order of: "Can't we skip filling out this form just this once? The customer is waiting" or "Aw hell, nobody's looked at these weight receipts for months. Let's skip it. I know you're in a hurry." As general manager, you and only you can replenish the supply of management control, and the only way you can do it is by your actions.

32

Learn to Cope with Vulnerability.

A BUSINESS EITHER GROWS or withers; the array of problems and opportunities is constant only in the briefest of periods. Hence, in order to maximize return on investment to the owners (and to ensure job continuity for the employees), a firm has no choice but to grow.

Growth is an adventure—it carries the firm into new product/service and geographical markets. It is a pioneering effort—crowned with rewards if successful but fraught with peril. But although everyone wants the rewards, only a few rare, genuine leaders are willing to incur the risk of failure.

The wrong kind of pride, the yearning to be fault-free,

is all too prevalent in management ranks. The mistaken notion that only errors of commission involve risks is too readily accepted. The premise of truly great leaders is: "There is so much more that I can do." Translating that premise into a criterion for managerial performance, acts of *omission* become as important as acts of commission. Failure to initiate action aimed at growth is a far more serious failure than running slightly over on expense budget in order to bring in a needed program.

An effective general manager *leads* the growth effort. As such, he will inevitably and almost always unfairly be judged with "20–20" hindsight. There is no way to avoid this price of leadership—you must be *vulnerable*. If you aren't, you are *not* performing the job for which you were hired.

Vulnerability to criticism is a condition of life for a general manager. It is the "heat" President Truman referred to.

An uncomfortable general manager is an ineffective general manager. Because constant vulnerability "comes with the territory," you had better learn early on to be comfortable while vulnerable, or your days as general manager will be numbered.

33

Get in the Batter's Box and Swing.
Babe Ruth Struck Out More Times
than Anyone Else, but He Also
(Until Hank Aaron) Hit More
Home Runs than Anyone Else.

EVERYBODY HAS A MIXTURE of love and respect for a "leader," an assertive "doer." What's more, everybody *needs* a leader: the parable of "one flock, one shepherd" cannot be taken lightly. Conversely, only disdain is accorded the "play-it-safe" Pontius Pilate. An effective general manager really doesn't need everybody's love; their respect will do just fine. And he certainly doesn't need disdain or, worse yet, indifference.

Manage for the long run. Capitalize on short-term opportunities and solve short-term problems, of course, but it's the long-term return to owners on which you'll be judged as a general manager.

As a general manager, you will over a period of time necessarily accumulate both correct and incorrect decisions: strikeouts as well as home runs. What matters, finally, is your batting record over a period of time. Will the effects of your correct decisions outweigh the effects of your incorrect ones?

Three factors determine the answer:

1. *Judgment:* Do you have the talent, experience, and patience required for good decision making? How's your batting eye?
2. *Decisiveness:* Do you have the courage to make decisions? Can you persuade others to accept them? Do you suffer from "paralysis by analysis"? Can you say yes or no? Are you willing to commit yourself— to swing the bat?
3. *Time:* Given the first two determinants present in requisite quality and quantity, all that remains is adequate time in which to play, so that the owners can compute a meaningful batting average based upon a sufficiently large data base. Will you have that time? How long will you be an active player?

34

Never Be Satisfied with Results.
Too Often, Profitable Companies
Become Comfortable Companies—
and Then They Are Profitable
No Longer!

THE YEAR HAS ENDED—the results are in, and you have exceeded every goal! What a tremendous feeling of accomplishment. You and your colleagues are generously congratulated, and deservedly so. You bask in the aura of success; it's truly an exhilarating experience. You'd like the recognition to go on and on.

But don't linger too long—another month is running

by and you'll soon face yet another management report. If the captain relaxes too long, the crew will go on vacation.

When you beat last year's results, all you really did was set this year's performance criteria another notch higher. And your first quarter this year had better exceed last year's first quarter, or else you'll be playing catch-up for nine months.

Pay no attention to years—that's only an accounting convention anyway. Plan and build your firm's growth on a quarter-by-quarter basis, regardless of which fiscal year a quarter happens to fall in.

Relentlessly pursue orders in excess of shipments, higher standard margins, smaller unfavorable variances, lesser expenses, smaller relative assets. You can *always* improve! If you see no prospects of progress from within —acquire! If you've established your dominant market position in the United States—go abroad!

Your work is never completely done! Thank God!

35

A Business Can Tolerate a Truly Enormous Number of Errors in Detail—if the Strategic Direction Is Relevant and Correct.

No PERSON OR ORGANIZATION has ever done or will ever do anything of significance in the most efficient possible way. All action must inevitably be *relatively* inefficient. It's only when the inefficiency level becomes intolerable that effectiveness, too, begins to suffer. And the inefficiency tolerance level of a business is surprisingly high. The profit margin for a new product may only be 31% instead of the planned 40%, but the firm will survive and continue profitably.

Of course, what a firm, as a business, *can* tolerate and what the owners of that firm are *willing* to tolerate are separate questions. The answer to the latter question lies in the specific situation. If your earnings forecast and dividend payout were premised on a 40% profit margin, then achievement of only 31% represents not inefficiency but ineffectiveness. You not only made a mistake, but you based your plans on that mistake. A geometrically proportional ratio is approximated between the tactical error tolerance and relevant strategic soundness.

None of this should in any way be interpreted to mean that we should condone errors. Errors reduce the positive end result. The important point for a general manager is that the sounder the strategy, the more numerous (and the more serious) the errors that can occur without unacceptably reducing profits.

The inference is obvious: it pays to invest proportionately more time in strategic rather than tactical planning.

36

Spectators Never Appear in the Record Books.

Do you *really* enjoy watching a football game, a baseball game, or a tennis match? Or would you rather be crossing the goal line, hitting the home run, or getting the ace yourself? The fact that you are only watching means that you either can not or do not want to be a performer. Yet somehow you derive vicarious joy. Perhaps you know that you could outperform them if only . . . (finish in your own twenty five words or less).

In the stadium of general management there are also spectator stands, and all too often they're jam-packed. If you're sensitive to Monday-morning quarterbacking, if you're content to be a faceless member of the crowd, if you prefer to remain invulnerable, stay in the stands. But if you thrive on contact, if you can ignore criticism by nonachievers, if you want to publicly measure your capability, then come on down into the arena—and take your chances.

Sure there is risk on the playing field, but there are proportionately greater potential rewards, too. The greatest of these is knowing that "I did it myself—my way." Through dedication, commitment, discipline, and considerable perspiration I made *my* mark, for all who come after to see.

It's only in the arena that you can feel the thrill of victory—or the agony of defeat. It is a greater fulfillment of human destiny, even in a short life, to enjoy the heights and survive the depths than to have merely existed, even for a considerable time.

37

Genuine, Meaningful "ROI" Improvement Is Generated Only by Corporate Growth.

You MEASURE A business firm's health the same way you measure an individual's. The specific readings of vital signs at one given moment or over a short time period are useless or even misleading. The behavior of the vital signs over a reasonable duration is the valid, true measure.

The most vital of all a firm's "vital signs" is, of course, Return on Investment (ROI). ROI is a fraction, equal to earnings divided by investment. The value of the fraction increases as the numerator (earnings) increases or the denominator (investment) decreases. Generally, the value of the numerator is a fifth or less of that of the denominator.

It's always easier to increase the numerator than to achieve a proportional decrease in the denominator, particularly as the numbers become large. After installation of prudent cost and expense controls, the only avenue open for earnings improvement is larger profitable sales volume. The notion of larger profitable sales volume can be summarized in one word—growth.

If you abandon the pursuit of growth as it is defined above and instead place primary attention on trying to improve ROI through asset reduction, you'll achieve a temporary and fleeting improvement; but the longer-term consequences will involve the ultimate asset reduction—liquidation

38

Avoid Becoming Responsible for Someone Else's Problems—You Should Have Enough of Your Own to Work On.

A "TAKE CHARGE" GUY wants to take charge. The more experience and training he has, the more he sees problems to be solved and opportunities to be exploited. He believes his involvement will contribute to positive results, so the temptation is to become involved. The ineffective manager will indeed become involved—here comes the rub—even if he is not held personally responsible for solving the problem or exploiting the opportunity.

As a general manager, you may encounter opportunities to become involved with subordinates, with other general managers (if there is a peer group in your firm), and with superiors. The temptation to become involved with the work of a subordinate occurs when the subordinate fails to perform his job well. He is either not solving his problems or not exploiting his opportunities—in short, he is not doing his job. The solution is to replace that subordinate. If you don't, you'll end up doing his job.

Getting involved with peers is venturing into very dangerous political waters. Involvement under direction from a superior incurs even more jeopardy, particularly if you're directed to proceed without public announcement or commensurate reward if predetermined goals are achieved.

Self-generated involvement will result in your performing work for which you were *not* hired. Do what you were hired to do.

39

Solving a Business Problem Always Generates Even More Problems.

PLEASED WITH YOURSELF, aren't you, now that your new-product plan has been approved? You faced a growth problem and solved it!

Or are you the chap who decided to improve cash flow this year by stopping all but maintenance and regulatory capital expenditures? Never mind what your competitors are doing—you're getting cash out, right?

It doesn't matter whether you're moving toward growth or toward liquidation: solving the problem at hand always generates new problems.

After the product plan has been approved, you still

have to face the problems of execution or implementation. Unanticipated reaction by competitors will test the plan's strategic soundness. You may be forced into ad hoc, tactical subsolutions which, as you may already know, will generate even more serious problems. (They're more serious because you must solve them under pressure, without benefit of prolonged and thoughtful analysis.) Inside your firm, faulty execution, misunderstanding, or even just plain incompetence will generate another wave of problems.

Mistaken emphasis on capital restriction to improve short-term cash flow merely trades off a current problem for future ones that will assuredly jeopardize the firm even more severely. Failure to invest on a sustained, programmed basis will ultimately increase the cost of your products or services and place your firm in a most unfavorable competitive position. The resultant decrease of revenues will, sooner or later, create cash flow problems of such enormity that Chapter 11 will seem an inviting option.

40

Master the Previous *Before* Leaping to the Subsequent.

WHY DOES A pro-football pass receiver fail to catch the ball just before turning upfield for a gain? Because he takes his eye off the ball? This only tells *what* happens, not *why* it happened. The reason he doesn't catch it is that he begins thinking about running with the ball before he successfully completes the prerequisite task of catching it.

How many times do you feel almost unbearable impatience with planning and yearn to "get on with the job," to "do something," to implement? "Let's get on with it–itis" is a disease that can doom you to failure. The higher the building, the deeper the foundation you need to keep it stable. Too shallow a keel helps swamp the vessel. Examples abound, yet only the effective general manager really learns from them.

Failure to master the "previous" before leaping to the "subsequent," failure to build a firm foundation before proceeding with the superstructure, is often cloaked in rationalization and compromise, especially when signals seem to say "Get on with it." All too often, subordinates will try to escape accountability by asking for more and more data before reaching a decision. Such behavior has been widely labeled "paralysis by analysis." The ineffective general manager, impatient to present the program to higher authority, will falsely accuse subordinates of paralysis-by-analysis. Responding to that accusation, the subordinates *will* promptly supply the program demanded, but it will contain an inordinate number of qualifications and conditions, such as "It is assumed that competitors x, y, and z will not retaliate during the product introduction period," and so on.

The larger the number of qualifications and conditions, the less the mastery over the "previous" that has been achieved.

The most insidious compromise occurs when you hear, "He's not the ideal guy for the assignment, but he's the best that we've seen so far and we're running out of time." It's better to delay than to settle for less than the best—better to postpone success than to ensure failure on schedule.

41

The First and Foremost Social Goal of a Business Is to Make a Profit.

CONSERVING THE ENVIRONMENT, bringing minorities into employee ranks by practicing prejudice-free recruitment and advancement, subsidizing employee education, broadening compensation benefits, adhering to the spirit as well as the letter of regulations—these are all commendable social goals. The problem isn't one of agreement or disagreement about that, but rather one of ranking. Resources are always limited; the issue is always allocation.

Unimpeded pursuit of enlightened self-interest will always produce lasting and desirable results. The first and foremost social goal of a business to make a profit —a profit just large enough so that owners' return on investment is sufficiently high to preclude disinvestment. The social and business goals of a business are identical.

Only an ample and consistent stream of profits will provide the wherewithal to even consider more than necessary spending or investment. Without profits, there is simply nothing to spend on community, ecological, or social projects. Without profits, the owners will liquidate and a firm's personnel will, sooner rather than later, swell the lists of the unemployed; and if the firm is large enough, its closing may generate a ripple effect among its suppliers. Failure to generate a satisfactory income stream, then, will ultimately abort any and all progress toward social goals.

If a firm fails owing to incompetence on the part of its management, it is a tragedy. If a firm fails because of untenable political or social incursions, it is a denial of the founding principles of America. It is an obscenity which must end in tyranny. It is a disavowal of free-market capitalism and a giant leap backward for mankind toward "big-brother" federalism which has an unbroken string of failure in man's recorded history.

42

Maintain Enough Constant Pressure to Expand Your Sphere of Authority.

YOUR SPHERE OF AUTHORITY, your sphere of influence, is a direct measure of your position in an organization. The larger the sphere, the stronger and more important your position. But remember, your sphere is flexible; it can expand or contract. Its size depends on two classes of forces: those outside the sphere (they tend to restrict or even shrink its size) and those inside. You and only you control these forces, which tend to maintain or increase its size. In the absence of inside forces equal to or stronger than outside forces, your sphere will fail to increase or may even shrink.

The outside forces exist permanently and exert themselves continuously. They include impersonal, macroeconomic developments and personal territorial-integrity pressures from others seeking to expand *their* spheres of influence.

The most powerful sphere *enlargement* force is simply *results*. Results consistently equal to or exceeding expectations not only equip you with impenetrable defenses, but also provide awesome offensive capability. Successful sphere expansion rests not on cute political tactics or power plays, but on consistent performance as an effective manager. Nothing succeeds like success.

43

No Superior Can Give You Authority. Your Extent of Authority Is Exactly What You Extract From Your Peers and Subordinates.

You've heard the old bromide, "Effective delegation requires that commensurate authority and responsibility be granted." What utter nonsense! Responsibility is something someone *assumes*—no one can grant it. Either a person *is* responsible and *will be* responsible, or he is not and never will be.

Effective delegation, then, demands that proper personnel selection and evaluation precede appointment so as to ensure that the person chosen will understand and willingly accept responsibility. Remember those in the service who consistently turned down corporal's stripes so as to avoid the responsibility involved? Many of them were qualified, even overqualified, as privates. But they did not desire responsibility, and they admitted it. Unfortunately, in business, such candor is rare.

Responsibilty is a character trait, but not so with authority! All but the rarest of us yearn for power in one manner or another. Organizational authority is merely an expression of that deeper need, and peers and subordinates know it. It's that recognition which enables resistance to take form. We resist someone else's authority because, if it is unchecked, our own power will diminish. We know that our authority, ultimately, is measured by the degree of surrender to us by peers and subordinates.

A positive and dynamic leader, however, can make this situation work productively. His *visible* recognition of individual dignity, his *publicized* expectation of excellence, his *observed* selfless dedication to problem solution rather than people manipulation, and his consistent adherence to achievement of results are critical to his effective use of leadership. His people will follow loyally —if they're convinced that their own future power will be enhanced.

44

The Numbers Can Never Be Too Hard.

THERE IS NOT ONE manufacturer anywhere in the world who knows what the actual cost of one of his products really is. There is not one financial results announcement of corporate performance that can unconditionally state what the exact profits are for that quarter.

Business numbers are generated by a firm's accounting system. At best, they represent the closest available approximations of the "real" numbers, based on generally accepted principles consistently applied, and approximations *must* necessarily be widely employed. Even calculations of month-end accruals are, at best, only averages or estimates.

The accuracy and reliability of business numbers, then, exist only to the extent that purposeful, dedicated effort is expended. Business numbers, then, always lack real-time and real-world accuracy. But the magnitude of the reliability gap is important. The goal must be to continually narrow that gap.

Business decisions are always *corroborated* by business numbers. A business decision based on an absence of numbers will be successful only by blind luck. The more that the supportive numbers can stand up to interrogation, scrutiny, and testing the better the chances that the resultant decision will be successful. As general manager, your interests are centered on making business decisions and on the validity, reliability, and relevance of the numbers which are the underpinnings of those decisions.

The audit report from your independent public accounting firm is only your first step toward obtaining hard numbers. Their report deals with tests of accounting practices and principles. But, the numbers you will seek to evaluate a decision alternative frequently lie outside the accounting system. They won't even get the scrutiny of an outside, disinterested professional. Examples abound: square foot availability, "cube" utilization in warehousing, plant capacity utilization, machine loading, tons shipped, forward aged order backlog data, number of orders or invoices or time tickets, and so on.

45

Don't Waste Your Time Risking Small Mistakes.

THE MOST CRITICAL INTERVIEW is the job interview. Selection of the right people to staff the firm's organization is an absolute prerequisite to success. No doubt you have a carefully developed interviewing style, but remember that the person you face also has one —an approach, or a series of questions and answers, uniquely his.

One question in a job interview that will tell you almost everything you need to know about an interviewee's managerial competence is, "What was the worst mistake you ever made; what was the worst damage you did to the P & L and Balance Sheet?" You immediately learn four critical things about a person from his or her answer. First, the magnitude of the mistake directly identifies the level that that person occupied in the decision-making hierarchy. You simply can't make big mistakes at low levels. And that magnitude also demonstrates the extent to which leadership was exercised. Furthermore, since few people repeat a mistake once made, you learn the depth of experience gained by the interviewee. Finally, the elaboration in the answer reveals character traits (especially the extent to which the mistake is palmed off as someone else's fault) and the extent of introspection practiced.

It is axiomatic that those who achieve great results concern themselves with great projects. Furthermore, great projects involve great risk. It is inevitable that those who succeed monumentally will have made monumental mistakes along the way.

Important results are never generated by trivial undertakings involving insignificant risk of failure. Get involved, therefore, only in activities where there is a risk of significant mistakes. It is only in such activities that you'll find the opportunity for significant achievement.

46

If Something Is Worth Doing, It's Worth Doing Imperfectly.

WE LIVE, AT BEST, in a 95% world. We seek perfection, but it successfully eludes all of us. Far too often, we achieve results well short of even the 95% level potentially available. But 95% isn't really all that bad!

You're in a sailboat in the middle of a lake and the hull springs a leak. Would you start reading a textbook on hull design so you could make a perfect repair in the hull? If you had done so in such a situation, odds are good you wouldn't be here reading this book today.

What you'd probably do, if you were an effective manager, is rush to stop 95% of the leak, organize a bailing crew to handle the 5% flow, inventory your resources, enumerate your alternatives, decide on one of them, and organize to execute it—while still monitoring the performance of both of the organizations you've established.

An obvious example? Perhaps, but how many times have you seen a general manager with declining profits, rising inventories and receivables, decreasing order input, or diminishing cash reserves fail to rush to plug 95% of the leak? Instead, he calls for another report, and yet another—until his reporting is so perfect that he can predict, with 100% accuracy, the month his firm will file for bankruptcy!

If expenses are too high, start to cut them *now*, when you get the first indications. Don't withhold action until you develop the perfect expense-reduction program. If inventory is too high, start cutting the input now; if receivables are too high, collect at least one past-due *now*. If you're in danger of blowing your profit target by $100,000, it's far better to miss it by $5,000 with imperfect programs than to miss it by $125,000 while you're developing the perfect program. And you're far better off capturing that new order at $950,000 than missing it while developing the perfect presentation for $1,000,000.

Above all, lead! By example, show your organization that you're not going to do a number on them if they only hit 95% on the first attempt. Half a loaf is not really all that much better than no loaf, but 95% of a loaf is nearly a whole loaf! It's enough to sustain you while you pursue the last 5%, if that last 5% is really worth the effort. (But remember: it just might be better to get another 95% loaf.)

47

Be Known to Have Ambition— Never Be Known as Ambitious.

THERE'S A WORLD of difference between Cassius and Horatio Alger. Not so much a difference in goals, really; rather, the differences center on the means they used to achieve essentially the same goal—personal success. Cassius pre-dated Machiavelli while Horatio Alger achieved one solid success after another by performing the job.

It's impossible to achieve lasting and worthwhile personal success at the expense of others. Sooner or later, one's reputation catches up with him. If that reputation is strewn with victims—or worse, is devoid of help ex-

tended to others—there will be great reluctance to en-
trust that individual with organizational and asset responsibility. Remember: time wounds all heels.

The mark of someone with ambition is easily discernible. Stated simply, it's the ability to build a team and lead
it to achieve the firm's goals. Leadership, a degree of
selflessness, competence, and integrity all are presumed,
too. Enthusiasm, lack of cynicism, and a reach toward
ideals provide the uplift and spark to mold and move an
organization.

To say that one must cultivate the proper image does
not demean the effort. Everyone, inescapably, projects
an image. To present the right image, one must first develop the right inner person.

In a business environment, the most easily recognized
earmark of ambition is a person's unswerving pursuit of
excellence. His commitment to perform his job better
than anyone else ever did, or ever will, will lead to outstanding results. A record of outstanding results will
lead, in turn, to a position of greater responsibility—a
promotion. A person with ambition will repeat the pattern again and again, in the same firm or in different
firms.

48

**A Decisive Man Will Always
Prevail, Only Because Almost
Everybody Is Indecisive.**

AN EFFECTIVE general manager must be decisive.
How many times have we heard that bromide? The
truth is, of course, that any manager, any leader, to be
effective, must be decisive. Decisiveness is not stubborn-
ness; it is not a posture. It is rather a willingness, after
prudent forethought, to act, to do. Decisiveness, per se, is
not a virtue. The action taken, the things done, are what
can make decisiveness a desirable trait. Decisiveness, per
se, is only an asset. The challenge is to channel and
direct the dynamism to further stockholder interests.

Everybody is willing to state an opinion, provided there's no contingent liability nor any requirement to act on that opinion. This is not decisiveness. Rather, decisiveness involves the notion of "putting your money (i.e., your job, career, or reputation) where your mouth is." It connotes self-confidence, integrity, and a willingness to endure the "slings and arrows of outrageous fortune." It's the willingness to both push *and* shove when push comes to shove.

This is not to say that every decisive person should prevail, or is a leader worth following. Rather, what is said is that a decisive person will prevail. Most people possess neither the self-confidence nor the assertiveness to take visible action in pursuit of a conviction. This unwillingness to act allows those who are willing to act to prevail.

But before you allow a decisive man to prevail, or loyally commit yourself to follow him, examine his characteristic patterns of action and the destinations toward which he leads. In short, exercise your own decisiveness.

49

An Effective General Manager Is an Expert Juggler.

THE EFFECTIVE general manager successfully balances functional interests and pressures, long- and short-term needs of the firm, internal and external developments, and lower and higher priorities. Factors of change exist both outside and inside the firm. These factors are incessantly active, always seeking to alter the status quo. Some of them are within the control of the general manager, others are not. Thus, the balancing or juggling act by an effective general manager successfully re-realigns priorities to serve the best long-term interests of the firm.

One thing is certain about the business environment:

it will change by tomorrow. There are simply too many external and internal forces at work to maintain the status quo. Competitors' actions or inactions, business decisions made by customers and suppliers, changes in the prime interest rate, and a host of other activities beyond your control change the external circumstances you face.

Performance by subordinates never equates to planned performance, either in timing or in results. Individual and, on occasion, collective decisions or actions by employees further affect planned results, favorable or otherwise. Occasionally, performance exceeds what you planned, but more frequently it doesn't meet published goals. Evaluation and reevaluation of all these developments are part of the general manager's job, but your responsibility goes beyond mere intelligence gathering. The accumulated data points must be interpreted to assay the net effect on the organization. More frequently than not, developments require corrective action to overcome their detrimental impact.

The selection and timing of remedial action requires further evaluation in terms of the firm's longer-range goals. You have limited resources at your disposal, so you'll constantly have to make allocation decisions. The ranking of priorities is *your* task. Usually, the reallocation of managerial resources, even for a short-term, task-force-type effort postpones completion of original assignments. You must keep all the balls in the air at the same time—and hoping that the curtain never comes down on your act in the absence of stockholder applause.

50

Never Propose Single-Vector
Strategy Plans.

No PLAN EVER PRODUCES everything it could, just
as no individual ever performs to his full potential. Final
results are always less than the delivered input. Execution, because of hostile outside forces and imperfect
internal action, always dilutes the impact of initial inputs. There are result levels, nonetheless, which are con-
sidered minimally allowable. You must ensure, then, that
your inputs exceed the minimum allowable results by as
large a margin as possible, even to the extent of overkill.

A vector connotes both direction and velocity. The
vector forces which act on an organization cumulatively

determine the direction and velocity which that organization will follow. Seemingly sound and deceptively simple, a running-scared directive to "increase sales" or "cut inventory," devoid of other considerations, will, if taken seriously by all subordinates, upset the vector-force balance of a firm and send it careening out of control.

As an effective general manager, any plan that *you* espouse *must* succeed. It must achieve, at least, minimum allowable results and show progress toward the firm's longer-range goals. Therefore, the effective general manager will formulate plans which not only provide sufficient resource deployment to exceed minimum allowable results, but which represent a balanced approach.

All measures of managerial or business performance are ratios. Changes in a ratio's value depend on changes in the numerator or the deonominator, or both. Since most of the denominators used in business (total assets, net assets, number of shares, total sales, etc.) are large numbers, it's often easier in business to increase the ratio's value by increasing the value of the numerator. But the value of the ratio can be *optimally* increased if the numerator is increased *and* the denominator decreased *simultaneously*. A single-vector plan, affecting either only the numerator or only the denominator, cannot begin to achieve optimum results—only a multivector plan possesses that potential.

51

For Firms That Intend to Stay in Business, Profit Plans Must Always Be Based on an Order Input Rate in Excess of the Sales Rate.

THE PERFORMANCE EFFECTIVENESS of a human being can be fitted to a curve throughout his lifetime. It begins at zero, increases slowly through adolescence, increases rapidly as meaningful experience is accumulated, peaks at some point, and finally decreases through old age, inevitably reaching zero once again.

The performance curve of a business firm can but need not duplicate the life cycle of a human being. Business firms either grow and flourish or atrophy and decay. They can never remain the same, maintain status quo, or fail to register the effects of forces acting upon them through the passing of time. It is better to grow and flourish than to atrophy and decay. A firm which grows and flourishes is contributing to the enhanced well-being of all human beings.

Business planning ought to reflect the intention of the firm's managers to have the firm grow. No firm can grow if its shipments are *planned* to exceed its receipt of new orders. If planned new orders do not exceed planned shipments, management has announced its intention to liquidate the firm.

There can be only one exception. When a firm embarks on a meaningful product-pruning program to correct past marketing practices, sales will generally exceed new-order input while backlog is sold off. Such an imbalance is acceptable if, and only if, planned volume of new orders will again exceed planned shipments in Planning Year Two.

52

If a Numbers Analysis Conflicts with Common Sense, Abandon the Numbers.

EFFECTIVE MANAGERS are constantly searching for numbers—numbers with which to eliminate adverbs and adjectives. To paraphrase, "One number is worth a thousand words." Basically, the need for numbers stems from the need for measurement. With numerical goals, you can not only measure the degree of achievement, but also keep track of interim progress. But *exclusive* dependence upon the numbers generated by the accounting system for the company books will lead, at best, to only partial measurements and at worst, to loss of control and ultimate failure.

There are many numbers that describe physical operational behavior. Pounds shipped, received, or moved through the plant, and many others, offer insight unavailable elsewhere. Expected future results must be expressed numerically or no justification for R & D, capital, new products, and other related projects would ever be approved. Accounting systems and prognostications are subject to managerial judgments. The question of allocation of costs and expenses is somehow resolved in every firm—no two of which are identical. Projections are subject to the extent and depth of knowledge and experience of the projector.

When numbers analyses are presented for your review and approval, insist that the numbers be translated into physical terms. Check the implications of the numbers in terms of people, floor layout, warehouse dimensions, heat, light, and power requirements, and security needs. These real-world insights will be major contributions to commonsense evaluations.

As general manager, you inevitably face the task of decision. You must ascertain whether the numbers offered you make sense, or whether they are too optimistic or too pessimistic. If they do not make sense to you, they will not make sense to the owners. Abandon them and get better numbers.

53

The Bigger the Decisions, the More Subjective the Decision-Making Process.

THE DEGREE OF SUBJECTIVITY called for in a business decision varies in direct proportion to the level of the organization layer involved in making decision. Decisions facing the lowest-ranking person in the lowest-ranking organizational layer require little interpretation and offer few alternatives. Much has already been predetermined; no new ground is being broken. No input is really expected from that individual—only output, defined as prescribed performance.

As we move up the organizational pyramid, however,

we encounter an increasing expectation for input, by the decision makers into the decision-making process. Procedure manuals become increasingly useless, and policy guides more pertinent. Less and less is it practical, or even possible, to enumerate the situations that will confront an individual. More and more judgment input is demanded.

Similarly, the higher the organizational level, the less one sees discrete, precise measurement—or, for that matter, any numbers at all. As higher-ranking individuals face decisions, they increasingly draw on nonroutine, one-time analyses or special reports. Furthermore, the higher the organizational position that one occupies, the closer one gets to the owner and the more conscious one is of the impact of any decision on the owner's equity value. That is, the higher one's position in the organization, the greater the impact of one's decisions on the firm's future course.

Most major decisions are made by the owners, and the most major decision they make, of course, is whether to invest (or continue investment) or disinvest. The more important the decision the further away is a ready supply of relevant quantitative data. More important to the success of the decision is the knowledge, background, competence, training, and experience of the decision maker.

54

At Best, Quantitative Analyses Only Justify an Already "Right" Decision.

THE EFFECTIVE general manager knows the "right" decision that will enhance stockholder equity. Just as an expert bridge or poker player has "card sense," a professional manager possesses "business sense." That intuitive decision-making ability comes from years of the right kind of experience—involving exposure to increasingly complex situations, increasingly frequent and intense vulnerability, and a healthy share of mistakes.

But the effective general manager does not rely solely on his intuitive business sense. While his intuition can and does, provide guidance and direction, the quantitative value of the investment decision at hand must be demonstrated to the board and the stockholders.

The vocabulary most readily accepted for justification and explanation is as devoid of words as possible and consists to the largest possible extent of numbers. Numbers can express changes in return-on-investment rates and much other critical shareholder data more succinctly and verifiably than words. Proceeding from quantified premises to a quantified projection of results, an explanation of the proposed plans or projects can be made with measurable precision. For, while there may be instant acceptance of the intuitive notion, approval to proceed can come only when numbers analyses are available for review and inspection.

Numbers can never replace professional managerial judgment. What they can do is complement that judgment, express it measurably, lend quantitative credence to it, and provide a vehicle for its effective communication.

55

Management Is Always a Contest of Wills—That's Why Persistence Always Wins.

A GENERAL MANAGER always wants his subordinates to do more, to extend themselves, to get more and better results. His effective subordinates have already extended themselves, because they are self-motivated. They naturally resist pressure for even further commitment. The less effective subordinates, fearful of any degree of vulnerability, initially offer only minimum commitment, which they're sure they can live up to. They, too, resist pressure for further commitment.

Prospective customers must be persuaded that your

products and services are indeed superior to those of your competitors. Your suppliers continually strive to improve their profitability position, and you continually strive to negotiate more favorable terms of sale. The adversary relationship so easily observed when dealing outside the firm exists within the firm to the same, and in some cases a greater, alarming degree.

A widely known, but seldom consciously employed, psychological principle is that of "diminishing response to a constant stimulus." When confronted by a seemingly unswerving, uncompromising, and relentless expression of will, it is entirely predictable that one will eventually view that expression as reality and modify one's behavior accordingly. Examples abound. The most devastating recent example was when Americans became tired of our involvement in Vietnam. We perceived that the Viet Cong and the North Vietnamese were relentless and untiring in their will to win. We gave up. *Persistence wears down opposition, and in the absence of opposition, one wins.*

The effective general manager, then, is perceived by his subordinates as unswerving, uncompromising, and relentless in the pursuit of excellence. That perception cannot be based on a mere image; it must reflect a genuine, deep personal commitment to excellence. Furthermore, the effective general manager wins *only* the contest of wills; he does not vanquish his subordinates. There are only two ways by which one wins any contest: graciously or ungraciously. The respect and loyalty of subordinates will be forthcoming in direct proportion to the graciousness with which you "win."

56

Never Just Attend a Meeting–
Always "Win" It.

GENERAL MANAGERS SPEND horrendous amounts
of time in meetings. Meetings, formal and informal, are
probably the most used, and abused, channels of communication in the business world. Nothing is so sad and
tragic as an opportunity unexploited or a gain unrealized.
It's the uncaptured potential of people who merely "attend" a meeting that people are subconsciously upset
about when they complain about there being too many
meetings.

A meeting is a gathering of opponents or competitors
(but hopefully not adversaries). Each brings to the meet-

ing a position, a set of priorities, some prejudices, and, generally, a defense aimed at lessening or at least maintaining his vulnerability. As such, a meeting is a contest —to see whether or not individuals can be persuaded to move from their positions, to realign their priorities, to overcome their prejudices, to extend their commitments, and to increase their vulnerability.

Enter a meeting, then, to win it. Do your homework, so that you are as well-armed as you can be. If the firm's goals and objectives are better served as a result of the meeting, you will have won. Focus the group's attention on key issues or developments as they affect the firm's prime goals and objectives. A win, after all, is not measured by the degree of change that you achieve in the participants, but rather by the degree to which the achievement of your firm's goals and objectives is enhanced.

Sometimes one hears classifications of meetings: some are merely to inform, some to make a decision, some to formalize assignments, and so on. In fact, there is only one purpose to every meeting—to enhance the prospects of achieving the firm's goals and objectives.

57

Become Immune to "Paralysis by Analysis."

A CRIPPLING AND USUALLY FATAL managerial af-fliction shows its first symptoms in such remarks as "We'll need further studies" or "The data are incomplete" or "There must be several alternative scenarios." And so on. The manager who incessantly pursues ever more data has somehow eluded the realization that decision making in business involves risk. While unnecessary or premature decision making must be studiously avoided, the attempt to completely wash away a decision by data inundation is easily and unerringly perceived as such by the organization. The only thing worse than a premature or unnecessary decision is an unmade decision.

On your way to becoming a general manager, you will observe the symptoms of "paralysis by analysis" among some of your peers. And at times you will see that they do, in fact, avoid their responsibility to decide; they avoid vulnerability. They seemingly escape, too, the Pontius Pilate label they deserve. They may even get away with it for extended periods, perhaps even for years. The problem? A weak superior who allows them to do a disservice to the firm—and to themselves.

Sooner or later, the weak superior will be replaced by an effective manager, and those subordinates who suffered from paralysis by analysis will be seeking other employment. The weak superior will be replaced because his function, or the firm, failed to meet owner expectations—which is the first disservice.

The subordinate who has departed faces the unpleasant task of writing a résumé. Prospective employers, of course, expect to read about "results achieved," but a victim of acute paralysis by analysis will have sucessfully avoided decisions, along with the concomitant commitment and vulnerability. The "results-achieved" section of his résumé will reflect a void in his managerial competence—which is the second disservice.

Too often, paralysis by analysis isn't incurred because of a desire to avoid vulnerability; rather, it's inflicted upon students in management schools where, too often, teachers and their students become excessively enamored of analytical techniques and procedures. They become bound up in the pursuit of efficiency and never achieve effectiveness. They lose sight of the purpose of data gathering and focus exclusively on the process.

Avoidance of vulnerability is at best an understandable motive. But to infect a potential manager at the outset with paralysis by analysis is not only unintelligible but inexcusable.

58

The More Someone Asks for
Supplemental Analyses the Less
Serious He Is
About Facing the Issue.

TOO MUCH OF A GOOD THING *can* hurt; indeed, too
much of a good thing can be fatal. Numerical analyses
are to a manager what glasses of water are to a thirsty
man. The first glass of water is treasured, the second
less so, and so on until the *n*th glass, which, when consumed, causes drowning. You can see this principle of
diminishing utility demonstrated in firms whose com-
puters spew forth tons of detailed data—all of which
are either dutifully filed or quietly discarded. Unfor-

tunately, they are never read or used. The quantity of data has passed beyond the nth quantum and threatens to drown management.

You can't escape accountability by saying no anymore than you can by saying yes. Both answers require justification and explanation. How do you signal that you opt not to proceed without so announcing? The ineffective manager vainly tries to escape vulnerability by use of the managerial "pocket veto." By requesting further and further analyses, he frustrates attempts to truly deal with an issue.

If the general manager allows it, a subordinate will successfully escape decision-making responsibility because of two unalterable principles: diminishing marginal utility and diminishing response to a constant stimulus. The effective general manager obtains only the minimum number of analyses necessary to fulfill obligations of communication and control. And he absolutely refuses to allow subordinates to equate performance with filled file drawers.

59

The "BS Content" in a Firm's Communication System Is Proportional to the Number of Layers in the Organization.

DID YOU EVER PARTICIPATE IN the parlor game in which a sentence is whispered from person to person? Try it. When the last person repeats the message it will invariably be far different from the original. Even under the best of conditions and with a universal intent to transmit with high accuracy, distortion does occur. .

In a business organization, the participants in the communication network operate neither under the best of conditions nor with a universal intent to transmit messages whole and without distortion. Conflicting motivations and the incomplete or incorrect perception of these motivations combine to produce distortion.

The "BS content" concept, however, refers to the amount of *intentional* message distortion. Every firm's communication network contains some BS content. Its presence doesn't reveal hostility toward the firm, its management, or its owners; rather, it reflects the need of the firm's employees for self-preservation and their cumulative disdain for vulnerability. They are seeking only to minimize the gap between their prior achievement and their commitment to future improved achievement levels.

A subordinate commits himself only to the minimum level of improvement acceptable to his superior. He will hold in reserve as much commitment as his superior allows him to. That superior will in turn discount the cumulative commitments of his subordinates when negotiating *his* commitment to *his* superior and will hold that discount in reserve.

Thus the "fudge factor" or BS content increases, layer by layer. The effective general manager never tries to dispel the BS content in his organization; rather, he *measures* it, subordinate by subordinate, and *controls* it. He does not allow it to result in commitment levels that are below those minimally acceptable to the owners. He may even contribute a measure of his own BS content so that the owners' expectations don't exceed what he believes, confidently, his organization can deliver.

60

Never Make a Decision Unless You Really Have to.

A PREMATURE BIRTH is far riskier than a full-term gestation. The more premature the birth, the greater the risk. A child needs a prescribed time in which to build up the elements—organs, tissues, systems—that he needs to successfully survive in an essentially hostile environment. If time to complete the development of the needed organizational strength is denied, the resultant weaknesses will jeopardize survival and may deny life.

The task of making decisions will be thrust upon you, as general manager, from many sources. Don't worry whether you'll have a chance to live up to the image of a dynamic, two-fisted decision maker: the buck does indeed stop at your desk.

Each decision that you make represents a time at bat and will affect your batting average. It will displease or even alienate someone or some group. Your effectiveness as a general manager exists only so long as you, through prudent decision making, stay below the threshold of displeasure or alienation levels. If you don't, the result is retraction of the authority granted you by subordinates. You will have lost the leadership position—you will have lost control.

Making unnecessary decisions only increases the risk of losing your control, your leadership position, and your effectiveness as a general manager. At best, you'll be viewed as a meddler rather than a manager. At worst, you'll have ruptured normal chains of command and confused the organization. Unnecessary decisions are always premature decisions, in the sense that insufficient time was invested in determining the need to make the decision. The normal required gestation period was cut short. Just as with a child, the more premature the birth or the less the amount of gestation, the more the risk to survival.

Making premature decisions increases the likelihood of making erroneous decisions. Your batting average will unnecessarily suffer. Your effectiveness as a general manager will vanish, not only from the viewpoint of the organization, but from the viewpoint of the owners as well.

Nothing Is as Effective as a Well-Planned Spontaneous Demonstration.

THE WELL-PLANNED spontaneous demonstration is a mighty management tool. A spontaneous demonstration is more persuasive, more compelling, than one which is obviously rehearsed, perhaps because the very element of apparent spontaneity somehow appeals to the heart and escapes the cynicism too often awarded more obviously cerebral efforts. It can be ill used, as it was by Josef Goebbels, the propaganda minister for Adolf Hitler. But it can also be used for good, and every effective general manager does indeed use it to further the growth and success of his firm.

The planning tasks for such a demonstration differ from most other planning tasks in at least two ways. First and foremost, they lack formal documentation. PERT and CPM charts, for example, would force such rigidity and formality that the spark of spontaneity would be destroyed. Assigning tasks and responsibilities would cast the participants as role players—a façade easily penetrated by the target audience. Informality must be the order of the day.

Management messages are routinely transmitted through formal channels of communication. But for a spontaneous demonstration, only informal communication channels are used. The effective general manager controls the "grapevine" in his organization. He does not fight it, try to eliminate it, or ignore it; he *controls* it so that it, too, can further enhance his firm's success. The effective general manager uses the informal communication system first to generate the expectation or anticipation of a coming demonstration and, second, to deliver the message which triggers it.

62

Use Approval-Level Sign-Off for Communication in All Operational Activities.

Too OFTEN, approval-level sign-offs are used only when processing capital expenditure requests. The effective general manager uses this technique in all operational activities—marketing, sales, engineering, personnel, purchasing, price and contract, and so on.

As general manager, you simply *must* know about all major developments and events in your organization. The effective general manager sees to it that he knows of developments or events *prior to* their occurrence. Their is no way that a general manager can remain adequately informed with anything less than a formalized, ritualized communication system.

Insist that *all* functions in your organization install a sign-off procedure to document all significant events or developments prior to their occurrence. The "waterfall" concept is most useful: successively higher tiers of management are required to sign off according to the impact (or potential impact) of the project or event on the firm's ROI. It is relatively commonplace to observe such a sign-off communication system used to publicize and control capital expenditures. In effectively managed firms, however, this technique pervades all impact-potential areas or activities.

The ineffective manager misinterprets this communication procedure: he views it as "red tape." He feels that he is forced to send every proposal "upstairs" for a *decision*. He fails to understand that the last thing that the effective general manager wants to do is to make all decisions. If the proposal documentation embodies a compelling profit-improvement demonstration, the decision has already been made! All that the general manager wants to do is stay fully informed.

In cases where resource limitation has been reached and allocations must be made, approval priorities will usually parallel the rates of ROI displayed by the array of proposed projects. In such a case, where capital is restricted, the "waterfall" sign-off technique ensures that all feasible alternatives are visible to the general manager so that the firm's proper priorities are served.

63

Nothing Is as Devastating to an Opinion as a Number.

JUST AS A SINGLE DART can annihilate a balloon, so a single datum can dispel the accumulated hot air of an ill-founded opinion. Consider the story of the upstart who terminated weeks of discussion about the number of teeth in a horse's mouth. Opinions and beliefs abounded; a plethora of theories issued forth. But it all came to naught when the upstart stood up, went to the stable, and—of all things—simply counted the teeth!

Thus, a single number was, and is, worth a thousand words. "How are orders going? How's business?" "Just fine. Really great." "As good as could be expected." "Pretty lousy." Do these remarks sound familiar? The answers are OK, I guess, when you casually meet business associates in an elevator, but they're never satisfactory when received from a subordinate in a formal meeting. If you, as general manager, take the time to ask, say, how new orders are going, you must settle for nothing less than a numbers answer. Adjectives and adverbs cannot be summed, subtracted, multiplied, and divided. They simply can't be measured or quantified at all. But with numbers in hand, you are fully capable of applying adjectives and adverbs.

What sort of numbers constitute an acceptable response? First, an actual current amount. Second, the standard to which the actual number should be compared. If the variance is significant, then the third required number is a prognosis and forecast of when and how the unfavorable or data point variance will be reduced or the favorable variance sustained.

Opinions are always self-serving. Numbers know neither masters nor alliances. Information flowing to you as general manager is sufficiently polluted with words. Seek out the numbers—filter the prose.

64

Every New General Manager Has
But One Honeymoon Period—
Use It Wisely.

AN OLD SAW, interminably quoted by practitioners
of the behavioral approach to management, is "People
resist change." That statement, in and of itself, provides
little useful insight for the new (or reborn) general
manager.

Resistance to change is a gray area, indeed. You'll
rarely encounter a vocal, visible demonstration of it;
it's almost always expressed by a growing disregard for
the *spirit* of existing rules and procedures, along with
a concurrent adherence to the *letter*. Other symptoms

include missed target dates, incomplete analyses, apathy, and an erosion of morale.

Resistance is magnified when a change is unexpected. Once a person has been conditioned to expect a change, the change itself is almost anticlimactic. Thus, an effective general manager will take the appropriate steps to prepare his organization for a planned change. A newly installed general manager, however, has a one-time opportunity to make changes without having to first condition the organization. The conditioning has already occurred, because everyone *expects* a new broom to sweep clean. The new general manager has a "honeymoon" period during which his personnel *expect* to see him put his personal imprint on the firm.

Several factors determine the length of the honeymoon period. If the firm's previous performance was poor, then not only will the organization expect change, but selective personnel will actually encourage change, and even suggest specific changes. Generally, the poorer the previous performance, the shorter the honeymoon period.

The tenure of one's predecessor is also a factor. The longer his tenure, the more satisfactory, presumably, was his performance, or else his tenure would have been shorter. Furthermore, the longer your predecessor held the office, the more the organization has been molded into a particular pattern. Conversely, the shorter his tenure, the less pervasive his influence. Generally, then, the shorter the tenure of your predecessor, the shorter the honeymoon period.

Finally, the size of the organization is an important factor. Organizations possess momentum; that is, they tend to continue on previous courses if change is not effected. The force of the organization's momentum is proportional to the number of individuals in the organization. Effective change requires effective communication, and the larger the organization, the longer the time period necessary in order to reach an adequate number of individuals so as to implement the change. Therefore, the larger the firm, the longer, generally, is the honeymoon period.

The honeymoon period does not last forever, so the effective general manager sees to it that key changes, at least, are implemented soon enough to beat the honeymoon deadline, but not so soon as to earn him the label of brash, impetuous, or insensitive. If changes are delayed beyond the honeymoon period, they will meet with much stronger resistance than if they had been made earlier. The expectation-of-change level of the personnel diminishes greatly after the honeymoon period; subsequent change will come as a surprise. The organization's adverse reaction is understandable. By allowing a change-free honeymoon you will have signaled, intentionally or not, that you endorse the conditions and personnel that you inherited. Thus, a later change amounts to repudiation and rejection—two attitudes which nurture, if not create, strong resistance.

65

Never Become Involved in the Personal Lives of Business Associates.

THERE'S A STORY about the New England minister who was holding forth from the pulpit. "Thou shalt not steal!" he thundered, and an elegantly dressed lady in the front pew answered, "Amen!" "Thou shalt not be slothful!" the minister continued. "Amen!" shouted the lady in the front pew. He went on, "Thou shalt not commit adultery!" This time the lady looked up and responded, "Hold on, Reverend, now you've stopped preachin' and you've started meddlin'."

As personal familiarity with subordinates increases, so does the temptation to meddle. It's inescapable—and potentially disastrous. If you hold a superior–subordinate relationship in your business roles, it is impossible to place that relationship in a drawer and act rationally in a personal relationship. The key to a truly successful superior–subordinate relationship is for the superior never to invade the "how-to" activity area, because personal relationships deal almost exclusively with "how-to" matters.

As a superior becomes personally involved with a subordinate, the latter will, inevitably, become resentful. The superior will soon label the subordinate an ingrate. These bad feelings will not remain submerged; they will eventually surface, even if unintentionally, within the business environment. As they do, the results both of you are accountable for will at best be jeopardized and at worst fail to materialize at all.

In summary, to the extent that you do become involved in the personal lives of your subordinates, you will at best diminish your objectivity, and at worst jeopardize your leadership position.

Management Planning Is a Two-Step Process: (1) Analysis—Defining in Detail the Objective(s), and the Tasks Needed to Achieve Those Objectives. (2) Synthesis—Ranking by Priority the Sequence of Specific Assignment of the Defined Tasks.

BUSINESS PLANNING IS as ineffective as it is because, unfortunately, it is a task all too often delegated (or relegated) to staff rather than line personnel. Not that the individuals engaged as staff planners are incompetent compared with line personnel—it's just that the content and substance of the planning task is alien to the staff function's data inputs and knowledge pools. There are portions of the planning process which can, and probably should, be assigned to staff. But assign staff overall control and responsibility, and the results will never be acceptable.

The first step in planning is the enumeration of objectives. More objectives are better than few; they provide a more complete description of the problem, thus furnishing added insights as to the tasks necessary to solve it.

When you first look over your list of objectives, you may be stunned by the apparent enormity of the problem facing you. It probably will be a rough one, but perhaps not as rough as you think. Take each objective and list the tasks necessary to accomplish it. Make the list as complete as possible, irrespective of timing and/or organizational responsibility. Ideally, the tasks will identify one-to-one with the objectives. In other words, by going through the formal planning process, you'll see that many of the objectives involve common task elements. Task C of objective #1 may prove to be task D of objective #2. Those common elements will help you maximize your effectiveness; but you'd never have discovered them if you hadn't gone the planning route.

Next, the objectives, along with the necessary tasks, must be priority ranked. You must make trade-off decisions. Suboptimization of one array to optimize another may be most desirable for the firm. Synthesis input should be limited to the data pool provided by analysis —this eliminates poorly thought-out ad hoc notions.

The board of directors that assumes that its prime role is to review results is asking for trouble. Its prime responsibility is the detailed and rigorous examination of plans.

67

The Right Answer at the Wrong Time Is Always a Bad Decision.

IN FRENCH COOKING, the sauce is everything. In business management, timing is everything. Taking action to grow, to retrench, to introduce a new product or abandon one may clearly be the right thing, in principle, to do, but unless your timing is right, the action to grow may be launched just prior to an economic peak, and a liquidity crunch will soon result.

Despite the hundreds of econometric models and the thousands of market projections completed every year, the future, alas, remains unknown. Probability curves and Delphic conferences notwithstanding, every busi-

ness decision must be made in anticipation of—but not
with certain knowledge of—future conditions, reactions,
or developments.

There are two phases to every business decision: pre-
launch and post-launch. During the pre-launch period,
all of the planning, evaluation, and "selling" (to the
board, to subordinates, to those affected) activities occur.
The post-launch period involves implementation—the
doing activity. Performance during both the pre- and
post-launch phases is a reliable measure of management
capability. Far too many decisions lead to undesirable
results because of management's failure to properly
maximize available controls during these two phases.

But the launch itself is another matter. Obviously,
management chooses the launch date that they feel is
best. But the selection of a launch date is the one decision element not subject to the same control and evaluation as pre- and post-launch elements. You can take
corrective action during both pre- and post-launch periods as unfavorable results surface. But once the launch
has occurred, it's impossible to "reverse the film" or replace the bird on the pad.

Effective monitoring of both pre- and post-launch
activity will quickly reveal the shortcomings of performance. Judgment of timing accuracy, however, can
almost invariably be made only after a considerable
time period. The longer the time period between launch
and data availability for judgment of that launch, the
closer the hindsight vision of Monday-morning quarter-
backs approaches 20–20.

68

There Are Really Only Two Types of Problems: Growth Problems and Liquidation Problems. Growth Problems Are Better.

BUSINESSES ALWAYS have problems; they vary only by number and complexity. It is the array of problems to which general managers should address themselves. Every firm possesses both growth and liquidation problems. Growth problems are generated by an active, effective manager. Liquidation problems are spawned by inaction and ineffectiveness. Because every manager is a mixture of action and inaction effectiveness and ineffectiveness, the results of his efforts must likewise be mixed. It is the balance (or imbalance) of the problems that matters. A firm never possesses only growth problems, but an occasional unfortunate firm does face only liquidation problems.

If a general manager allows liquidation problems to command more and more of the board's attention, it's time to find a new general manager. Perhaps a useful measure of the effectiveness of a general manager is the ratio of growth to liquidation problems that he generates during his tenure.

If, on the other hand, the board (representing the interests of the owners) initiates more and more liquidation problems, it's time for an effective general manager to depart. The future of the firm is behind it.

Unless a general manager maintains a reputation for growth, he will establish a reputation for liquidation. The market is extremely limited for a general manager with a proven record of liquidating firms.

69

Constantly Test the Ranking of Planned Action Priorities.

ACTION PLANS are formalized, documented, and priority-ranked during preparation of the firm's budget plan, profit plan, or business plan. In other words, they are priority ranked some three to six months before the beginning of the fiscal year in which they are to be implemented. Put yet another way, the assigned priorities may be a year old or more by the time that they are put into effect. During the elapsed time, many developments, both internal and external, have affected those plans or the results you anticipated from their implementation.

The ultimate goal of every planned action is improvement of stockholders' return on investment. The extent of that improvement will vary according to the specific planned action. Anticipated ROI will vary, through time, even with respect to the same planned action. As internal and external forces and developments generate their individual and cumulative effects, the actions planned a year or more ago will certainly be affected, favorably or otherwise.

During the time interval of up to two years between original project identification and selection and the end of Planning Year One (the planned implementation period), new projects should be formulated. They will be generated by the abundance of opportunities which appear to every firm during a two-year interval. The decision to proceed or not with a new planned action can be made intelligently and effectively only if the anticipated results are compared to the results of previously approved planned actions.

Thus, competition for limited resources is affected not only by changes surrounding planned actions previously approved, but also by the claims put forth for new proposed actions. In the absence of continuous surveillance and monitoring of the firm's priority ranking, your limited managerial and capital resources will be misallocated; that is, you will commit them to tasks and projects that no longer offer promise of optimum results. The moving finger will write and, having writ, move on; and all of your task forces and all of your crash programs will be unable to alter its message one bit.

70

When Nothing Else Works...

THERE WILL BE moments when, despite all the training and experience that you've acquired, you will need help—maybe not technical or quantitative help, but inspirational help. It's really not a bad idea to start each business day by renewing your awareness of your need for these qualities:

Please, God, grant me—
- *The spark to imagine*
- *The daring to innovate*
- *The discipline to plan*
- *The skill to do*
- *The will to achieve*
- *The commitment to be responsible*
- *The leadership to motivate*

ABOUT THE AUTHOR

RICHARD S. SLOMA has had a distinguished career in management. He has been: Division President of I.T.T.; President of Bastian-Blessing, Inc.; Division President, Executive Vice President C.O.O.; and President, C.E.O. of Golconda Corporation. He is a member of the Institute of Management Sciences and the Presidents Association of the American Management Association.

MONEY TALKS!
How to get it and How to keep it!

☐	22936	HOW TO GET FREE TAX HELP by Matthew Lesko	$2.95
☐	23455	YOU CAN NEGOTIATE ANYTHING by Herb Cohen	$3.95
☐	23160	GUERRILLA TACTICS IN THE JOB MARKET by T. Jackson	$3.50
☐	20952	THE ONLY INVESTMENT GUIDE YOU'LL EVER NEED by Andrew Tobias	$3.25
☐	23453	HOW TO WAKE UP THE FINANCIAL GENIUS INSIDE YOU by Mark Oliver Haroldsen	$3.50
☐	20296	THE COMING CURRENCY COLLAPSE: And What You Can Do About It.	$3.95
☐	20387	COMPLETE MONEY MARKET GUIDE by Wm. Donoghue	$3.50
☐	20478	THE COMPLETE BOOK OF HOME BUYING by M. Sumichrast & R. Shafer	$3.95
☐	23099	THE GAMESMAN: The New Corporate Leaders by Michael Maccoby	$3.95
☐	20613	THE GREATEST SALESMAN IN THE WORLD by Og Mandino	$2.50
☐	22550	ALMOST EVERYONE'S GUIDE TO ECONOMICS by Galbraith/Salinge	$2.95
☐	20191	HIGH FINANCE ON A LOW BUDGET by Mark Skousen	$2.95
☐	22672	GETTING RICH: A SMART WOMAN'S GUIDE TO SUCCESSFUL MONEY MANAGEMENT by Diane Ackerman	$3.95
☐	22569	HOW TO BUY STOCKS 6th ev. ed. by Louis Engel	$3.95

Buy them at your local bookstore or use this handy coupon:

Bantam Books, Inc., Dept. MSP, 414 East Golf Road, Des Plaines, Ill. 60016

Please send me the books I have checked above. I am enclosing $_____
(please add $1.25 to cover postage and handling). Send check or money order
—no cash or C.O.D.'s please.

Mr/Mrs/Miss_____

Address_____

City_____State/Zip_____

MSP—2/83

Please allow four to six weeks for delivery. This offer expires 8/83.